1 Corinthians

Brian Harbour

Also by Brian L. Harbour

17 Roadblocks on the Highway of Life and How to Move Around Them

Jesus the Storyteller: Relating His Story to My Story

Praise for *Preaching the Word: 1 Corinthians*

Dr. Brian Harbor offers to us in this contemporary contextualized pastoral treatment of 1 Corinthians just what we have come to expect from him for a generation. Generous in pastoral wisdom, apt in memorable anecdotes, accessible in narration of the text—these characterize his able biblical exposition. He joins the past historic situation of Corinth with the present situation of today's church in an energetic and engaging conversation. To merge the horizons of long ago with the horizons of today is no easy thing and he has done this in a fresh way. This book is truly a text message for right now.

—**Joel C. Gregory**
Professor of Preaching, George W. Truett Theological Seminary
Baylor University
Distinguished Fellow
Georgetown College

I have great respect and admiration for my friend Dr. Harbour, and he has led several very successful churches for over forty-plus years. I have always had a deep interest in 1 Corinthians, and as a Sunday school teacher, I see this book as an excellent tool and resource. It will help me in my efforts to share God's word.

—**Drayton McLane**
Chairman of the McLane Group and
Chairman/CEO of the Houston Astros

Brian Harbour combines the best of critical scholarship with practical insights for weekly preparations. This commentary fills a critical gap between the library and the pulpit, offering contemporary application with depth and clarity.

—**William D. Shiell**

Smyth & Helwys Publishing, Inc.
6316 Peake Road
Macon, Georgia 31210-3960
1-800-747-3016
©2018 by Brian L. Harbour
All rights reserved.
Printed in the United States of America.

The paper used in this publication meets the minimum requirements of
American National Standard for Information Sciences—
Permanence of Paper for Printed Library Materials.
ANSI Z39.48–1984. (alk. paper)

Library of Congress Cataloging-in-Publication Data

Harbour, Brian L.
First Corinthians / by Brian Harbour.
p. cm.
Includes bibliographical references.
ISBN 978-1-57312-908-4 (pbk. : alk. paper)
1. Bible. N.T. Corinthians, 1st—Commentaries.
BS2675.53 .H34 2017
227/.207—dc23

2016056022

Disclaimer of Liability: With respect to statements of opinion or fact available in this work of nonfiction, Smyth & Helwys Publishing Inc. nor any of its employees, makes any warranty, express or implied, or assumes any legal liability or responsibility for the accuracy or completeness of any information disclosed, or represents that its use would not infringe privately-owned rights.

Dedication

C. W. Christian, Bob Patterson, and Glenn Hilburn,
Baylor professors
who nudged me along the pathway of learning

Contents

Preface	ix
1. When Christ Meets Culture	1
2. Fully Equipped	5
3. No Us and Them in the Church	11
4. The Message of the Church	17
5. God Works in Mysterious Ways	21
6. Jesus Christ and Him Crucified	27
7. The Wisdom of Christ	33
8. Worldly Christians Versus Spiritual Christians	39
9. The Foundation of the Church	45
10. All Things Are Yours	51
11. Found Faithful	57
12. Fools for Christ	63
13. Motivations for Ministry	69
14. Weeds in God's Garden	75
15. The Church's Image	81
16. Right and Wrong	87
17. Christian Marriage	93
18. Remain As You Are	99
19. You Don't Have to Be Married to Serve God	103
20. Christians Who Are Christian	109
21. The Myth of Unlimited Freedom	113
22. The Church Is Not about Meeting My Needs	119
23. Learning from History	125
24. Two Inescapable Truths about the Christian Life	129
25. Choosing Sides	133

26. Absolutes and Nonessentials	139
27. The Right Attitude in Worship	145
28. Experiencing True Fellowship in the Church	151
29. The Gifts of the Spirit	157
30. Spiritual Gifts and the Church	161
31. What's Love Got to Do with It?	167
32. The Gift of Tongues	173
33. Orderly Worship	179
34. The Resurrection of Christ	185
35. The Resurrection of the Dead	189
36. The Interception of Entropy	193
37. What's the Deal with the Offering Plates?	199
38. Opportunities and Obstacles	203
39. A Door into a New World	207

Preface

Two consistent appeals inspired this book. The first is the appeal for "biblical" preaching.

People are hungry for the strong meat of God's word, and they want more than just a verse of Scripture that provides the platform from which a preacher jumps into a favorite spiritual theme. They want to understand the broad sweep of the biblical message. They want to struggle with the difficult texts as well as the simple texts. They want to know how God's word—all of it—intersects with their lives today.

Matching that appeal for sound biblical preaching is the desire for direction in relating the church to the changing world around us. Christians today, especially young Christians, embrace the mission mindset. They want to be a part of what we refer to as "missional" churches. Driven by the incarnational principle, they want to know how to contextualize the church in today's culture. What better way to demonstrate biblical preaching than to take an in-depth look at an entire biblical book, and what better example of a church trying to contextualize the gospel than the church Paul planted in the corrupt, worldly, pluralistic city of Corinth?

These two appeals inspired me to put together what I am calling a "homiletic commentary." This book is a commentary in the traditional meaning of that word, a critical explanation or interpretation of a text, for I will examine every part of Paul's letter we know as 1 Corinthians and seek to explain and interpret these texts. However, my approach will not be that of a New Testament scholar but that of a preacher. Each of these chapters began as a sermon preached to the First Baptist Church in Richardson, Texas, and I also preached most of them to the First Baptist Church in Waco, Texas. I do not follow the traditional deductive approach that begins with a summary of the text's meaning and then deduces some ideas from that summary, usually spelled out in specific points and often decorated with alliteration. Instead, these sermons are more inductive, unfolding around a series of questions asked of the text. I do some enumeration along the way and occasionally even fall into alliteration. But mostly, these sermons follow what I call the developmental style of preaching. While the style and the illustrations likely will appeal more to a Christian in the pew than to a scholar at a desk, I hope the messages will nevertheless provide a meaningful explanation and interpretation of the text we know as 1 Corinthians.

When Christ Meets Culture

1 Corinthians 1:1–3

The most significant idea in the opening words of 1 Corinthians is not that this letter is written by Paul, that God called Paul to be an apostle, that the Christians at Corinth have been set apart to live holy lives, or that Paul offers to these first-century believers the grace and peace of God. The most significant idea in the opening words of 1 Corinthians is that Paul writes these words to Christians who have to live out their lives "in Corinth."

These first-century Christians in Corinth are kingdom citizens who have to live in a Roman world. Spiritually they are in Christ, but geographically they are in Corinth. The context of the Christian life, not only in the first century but also in every century, has been the dynamic tension between the church and the world, between Christ and culture.

How do Christ and culture intersect? In 1951, H. Richard Niebuhr presented some answers to that question in his book *Christ and Culture*. Niebuhr identified four different ways in which the Christian church relates to culture. He described Christ against culture, the Christ of culture, Christ above culture, and Christ the transformer of culture.1 I studied those suggestions from Niebuhr again recently and found them still relevant and helpful, but I want to suggest a simpler approach. I believe the church has three alternatives in relation to culture: isolation, identification, or incarnation.

Following the strategy of *isolation*, the church withdraws completely from the world. This strategy provides some protection for the church and distances the Christian from the evil influences of the world. However, this approach removes the church from the world so much that although the church has something to say to the world, the church has no channels by which to communicate that message.

Following the strategy of *identification*, the church becomes completely engaged in the world. This strategy gives the church multiple connections with the world. However, such links with the world have a way of becoming sponges by which the church absorbs the mind-set and attitudes of the world. In this viewpoint, even though the church has channels by which to communicate its message to the world, the church becomes so much like the world that it no longer has anything significant to say.

The third strategy, *incarnation*, places the church in the world but reminds the church constantly that it does not belong to the world and is in fact distinct from the world. *In* the world but not *of* the world—that is the strategy of incarnation.

That the first Christians followed the strategy of incarnation is not distinctly articulated but is clearly implied by the images of the church in the New Testament. Jesus provides the primary model for this strategy, and he instructs us to follow a similar strategy. "As the Father has sent me," Jesus tells the disciples in John 20:21, "I am sending you." Jesus became flesh and dwelled among us in such a way that we can see in him "the glory of the One and Only, who came from the Father" (John 1:14); in the same way, the church is to dwell in the world in such a way that the people of the world can see in us the glory of the One and Only who came from the Father. Christians in the world but not of the world, Christians who live as kingdom citizens in the world, *incarnation*—that is the New Testament strategy.

What happens when the church follows this strategy of incarnation? First Corinthians provides an answer to that question. When Christ intersects with culture through Christians who incarnate the gospel in their world, it is a messy, confusing, divisive, challenging, and sometimes discouraging proposition. Contextualizing the gospel into this fallen world is messy!

Paul discovers that truth when he takes the gospel to Corinth in the first century. A list of the significant cities of the Roman Empire in the first century includes the city of Corinth. Strategically located on the isthmus that connects the northern and southern parts of Greece, Corinth had become a major crossroads. All north/south traffic passed through the city of Corinth. Corinth's position on an isthmus also enabled it to become a passageway for east/west traffic that arrived by ship from the east, moved through Corinth to the west, and then ended up on another ship. Corinth's strategic location contributed to its economic prosperity. People from every tribe and nation visited the markets of Corinth. With the heavy flow of merchandise passing through the city, Corinth developed into one of the commercial centers of the ancient world.

Since the strategic location and economic prosperity also made Corinth the logical choice for the political base in the area, Corinth became the capital of the Roman province of Achai. The presence of the Roman military and the Roman proconsul who resided in Corinth added to the city's prestige. In such an environment, buoyed by financial abundance and laced with political intrigue, immorality found fertile soil. In fact, rather than opposing immorality, the worship of Aphrodite, the love goddess, sanctioned immorality, and in the temple to Aphrodite, one thousand cult prostitutes played a central role in the regular routines of worship.

Pluralistic, multicultural, urban, profane, political, and immoral—all of those words describe the Corinth of the first century. Paul and the first-century Christians can choose to isolate themselves from that environment and settle into a Christian camp out in the wilderness, or they can establish an intimate connection with that environment that will obliterate their distinctiveness. Instead, Paul gives a handful of believers the messy, confusing, divisive, challenging, discouraging responsibility of incarnating Christ in the city of Corinth. Paul and the Corinthian Christians reject the strategies of isolation and identity for the strategy of incarnation. They are kingdom citizens who have to live *in Corinth* (v. 2).

How do they carry out this assignment? When we consider the text, we see that these first-century Christians called to live as kingdom citizens *in Corinth* have several things going for them.

First, they have a *connection*. These Christians in Corinth are *sanctified in Christ Jesus* (v. 2).

A cartoon shows a guidance counselor going over the results of an aptitude test with a student. As he reviews the results, the counselor informs the student, "The results of your test indicate that you should seek employment with a company where your father has an influential position."

That is the secret of the Corinthian Christians—not that they are so talented, not that their faith is so strong, and not that they have such vision. Their secret is that they are employed in a business where their heavenly Father has an influential position. They are connected with God through Jesus Christ, and that connection keeps them going.

They also have a *community* to which they belong. These Christians in Corinth are a part of *the church of God . . . together with all those everywhere who call on the name of our Lord Jesus Christ* (v. 2).

A man driving down a country road in the rain slips off the road into the ditch. A farmer standing nearby with his mule, Buddy, offers to pull him out of the ditch. The farmer hitches Buddy to the rear bumper of the car and shouts, "Come on, Nellie, pull!" Then he shouts, "Come on, Buster, pull!" And then he adds, "Come on, Coco, pull!" Finally he leans over to Buddy and whispers, "Come on, Buddy, we need you to help pull the man's car." With that, Buddy pulls the car out of the ditch. The driver says to the farmer, "That is really strange. Why did you call your mule all those wrong names before calling him by his right name?" "Buddy is blind," the farmer explains, "so he can't see what's going on around him. But if he thought for one moment he has to do this all by himself, he would never have pulled your car out of the ditch."

Again, that is the secret of the Corinthian Christians—not that they are so talented, not that their faith is so strong, and not that they have such vision. Their secret is that they do not have to carry out their assignment all by themselves. They have each other. They are part of a community of faith, and that community keeps them going.

Third, they have a *covering*. They live out their lives in the context of God's *grace and peace* (v. 3).

In a Dennis the Menace cartoon a few years back, Dennis and his little friend Joey leave Mrs. Wilson's house with their hands full of cookies. Joey says, "I wonder what we did to deserve this." Dennis answers, "Look, Joey, Mrs. Wilson gives us cookies not because we're nice, but because she's nice."

That is the secret of the Corinthian Christians—not that they are nice but that God is nice. They are blessed by the grace and peace of God, and that blessing from God keeps them going.

The challenge confronting the Christians in Corinth in the first century confronts us Christians here in our communities in the twenty-first century. We too are kingdom citizens who have to live in a pagan world. We too have been called to contextualize the gospel in our community through the strategy of incarnation. And we too will find that assignment to be messy and confusing and divisive and challenging and discouraging. Yet if we stay connected to God and to each other and if we depend not on our own strength but on the grace and peace of God, we can do it. For the world's sake, we must do it.

Note

1. H. Richard Niebuhr, *Christ and Culture* (New York: Harper & Row, 1951).

2

Fully Equipped

1 Corinthians 1:4–9

Arguably the greatest coach in the history of the National Football League was Vince Lombardi, legendary coach of the Green Bay Packers. What made him such a great coach? Opinions differ on that question, but at the heart of the answer is the way he prepared his players for the game each week. Bart Starr, perhaps the Packers' most famous quarterback, testified to this dimension of Lombardi's coaching genius. Coach Lombardi met with his quarterbacks every Wednesday, Thursday, and Friday morning—not just with Bart Starr but with all of them—to develop and refine Sunday's game plan. By the close of Friday's meeting, the quarterbacks understood the game plan perfectly and felt prepared for every contingency. Nothing was left to chance. Bart Starr later affirmed that he was so thoroughly prepared that he knew he would never face a situation he was not equipped to handle. He still had to react to the game situation, and he still had to carry out the plays, but Coach Lombardi gave him everything he needed to carry out the game plan and win the game.[1]

Paul says much the same thing to the Christians in Corinth as they face the challenging task of contextualizing the gospel in the culture of that first-century city. We see his word of assurance in verse 7: *Therefore you do not lack any spiritual gift as you eagerly wait for our Lord Jesus Christ to be revealed.* Paul assures the Corinthian Christians that God gives them everything they need to carry out their assignment "in Corinth." They are fully equipped.

What does God give them?

First, God gives them the tools they need to contextualize the gospel in their community. *For in him,* Paul writes in verse 5, *you have been enriched in every way.* Paul moves immediately from this general pronouncement—*in every way*—to identify two particular manifestations of God's enrichment in their lives. God enriches them in their "speaking" (*logos*) and in their "knowledge" (*gnosis*). *Logos* probably refers to the different gifts of speech mentioned in 1 Corinthians 12—14, and *gnosis* probably refers to the gift of prophetic revelation cited in 1 Corinthians 12:8. The Corinthian Christians have been enriched with the gifts of speech and knowledge.

As we will see in later parts of the letter, the Corinthians sometimes abuse these gifts by exalting their words over the words of the cross (1:17-18) and by exalting their gift of knowledge over love (8:1-3). Most commentators correctly recognize in Paul's statement a backhanded jab at the Corinthians, reminding them that these gifts of which they are so proud come from God. But on the positive side, Paul confirms that God provides all the spiritual gifts the Corinthian Christians need to carry out the task of being the church in Corinth. Whatever they face, the Corinthian Christians are prepared for it. They have the tools.

In addition, God assures the Corinthians that they will be victorious in their endeavor. *He will keep you strong to the end*, Paul writes in verse 8, *so that you will be blameless on the day of our Lord Jesus Christ*. The phrase *on the day of our Lord Jesus Christ* refers to the final judgment, and the promise of Paul to the Corinthian Christians is this: on that day God will welcome them into his presence and will judge them to be blameless and acceptable. This is an amazing promise to the members of the most corrupt, divided, and at times disappointing group of Christians we read about in the New Testament. Paul's confidence, of course, rests not in the Corinthians but in God, for they will win the game and stand ultimately triumphant before God not because of their strength but because of God's strength. God will keep them strong to the end. God has prepared the Corinthian Christians for whatever they will face, and Paul assures them that his game plan will work and that they will ultimately be victorious.

In addition, God gives them a great coach. In verse 9, Paul writes, *God . . . has called you into fellowship with his Son Jesus Christ*. Down through the years, in every sport, some people have earned recognition as men and women who simply know how to coach. Year after year, with different individuals, they continue to win. Opposing coaches used to say about Coach Bear Bryant at the University of Alabama, "He can take his team and beat yours and then he can take your team and beat his." Some people just know how to coach. But can you imagine playing the game of life with Jesus as our coach, with Jesus making the game plan, and with Jesus calling the plays? Paul reminds the Corinthians that this is exactly what they have going for them. God calls them into fellowship with his Son Jesus Christ, and as they carry out their assignment for him, Jesus leads the way. Jesus shows them how to live. Jesus is their coach.

Here is the conclusion from our text; these Corinthian Christians have the tools they need to carry out God's game plan, they have the assurance of victory as they carry out that game plan, and they are a part of a team of believers with Jesus as their coach. God gives the Corinthian Christians everything they need to carry out his game plan and to make an impact on the world. That is the promise of our text.

This passage not only describes First Church in Corinth in the first century but also our churches in the twenty-first century. God has the same game plan for us as he did for the Corinthians. He wants us to contextualize the gospel in our communities through the strategy of incarnation. Likewise, God has given to us the same manifestation of his grace that he gave to the Corinthians. He has given us the tools to carry out the game plan, the assurance of victory as we carry it out, and a great coach to guide us. God has given us everything we need to carry out his game plan and to make an impact on our world for him.

Several years back, the journalist-writer Fred Bratman asked author and speaker Henri Nouwen to help him understand how he could live a spiritual life in the midst of a secular world. Nouwen responded with one of his simplest and yet most powerful books, *Life of the Beloved.* This book affirms simply that we are beloved by God. That, Nouwen explains, is the foundational truth of the spiritual life. Whatever happens, Nouwen concludes, a voice speaks from above and from within and whispers softly or declares loudly, "You are my Beloved; on you my favor rests."[2] Nouwen is talking about us. When we look at ourselves in the mirror every morning, we should also hear that voice: "You are my Beloved; on you my favor rests." Every time we gather for worship, that same assurance should reverberate through the room: "You are my Beloved; on you my favor rests." God has given us everything we need to carry out his game plan and to make an impact on the world. Let me give two illustrations of that truth.

Several years ago I heard about a woman who was deeply spiritual and who recognized the generosity of God, despite her sometimes difficult circumstances. In one of those dark nights of her life, she ran out of money and had nothing to eat, so she got down on her knees and prayed, "God, you promised to take care of me, and you have done this over and over again. So I am asking you to do it again by sending me a loaf of bread so I will not starve." At that moment the local atheist passed by her house, and, since in those days the windows were usually open, he overheard her prayers. He recognized this to be a great opportunity to mock the old woman's faith in a generous God. Later that day he got a loaf of bread, crawled up on her roof, and dropped the loaf of bread down her chimney. He then listened outside as she joyfully thanked God for answering her prayer. The atheist knocked on her door, and when she opened it, he informed her with a scornful laugh that it was not God but he who had given her the bread. Without missing a beat, the woman responded, "You are wrong. God provided the bread, even if he did use the devil to deliver it." That woman echoes the declaration of our text: God has given us everything we need to carry out his game plan and to make an impact on the world.

Saint Patrick, Ireland's patron saint, often started his day with this confident prayer:

> I arise today with
> The power of God to guide me
> The might of God to uphold me,
> The wisdom of God to teach me,
> The eye of God to watch over me,
> The ear of God to hear me,
> The word of God to give me speech,
> The hand of God to protect me,
> The way of God to prevent me,
> The shield of God to shelter me,
> And the host of God to defend me:
> Against the snares of the devils,
> Against the temptations of vices,
> Against the lusts of nature,
> Against every man who meditates injury to me,
> Whether far or near, with few or with many.[3]

Should this be our prayer each morning as we face the new day before us? God has placed us in a local church in the midst of our postmodern, pluralistic, and often immoral world and has given us an unmistakable mission—we are to contextualize the gospel in this city. The good news is that God has given us everything we need to carry out that assignment. We are fully equipped.

How should we respond to this challenge? Well-known Baptist and later Episcopalian preacher John Claypool presents an intriguing image in his little book *Stages: The Art of Living the Expected*. He suggests that children need to be given "a Christmas-tree spirit" about themselves. Someone, he explains, needs to point out to our children the packages of potential and opportunity that God has placed in their lives and encourage them to unwrap, discover, and develop these gifts.[4]

I believe our text suggests that all Christians need to have a "Christmas-tree spirit" about our work as God's people. We need to realize that within each of us God has placed packages of potential and opportunity, and it is our privilege—even more, our responsibility—to unwrap, discover, and develop these packages. They are God's gifts to us to equip us to carry out his kingdom work in the place where we live. Remember that it will be messy, and it will not always be easy. But we can be sure of this: we are fully equipped for the task. That is the promise of God's word.

Notes

1. Michael O'Brien, *Vince: A Personal Biography of Vince Lombardi* (New York: William Morrow and Company, 1987) 237.

2. Henri J. M. Nouwen, *Life of the Beloved* (New York: Crossroad, 1992) 28–29.

3. Ken Gire, *Reflections on the Word* (Colorado Springs: Chariot Victor Publishing, 1998) 24.

4. John Claypool, *Stages: The Art of Living the Expected* (Waco: Word Books, 1977) 29.

3

No Us and Them in the Church

1 Corinthians 1:10–17

In one of his lesser-known essays, C. S. Lewis deals with a common experience in human society. The title of the essay was "The Inner Ring." According to Lewis, two different systems exist in every organization. One is a formal system with specifically identified positions and an easily recognized structure. The other is an informal system that is never identified in any manual, that is never formally organized, and to which a person is never formally admitted. Yet it is clear to anyone with perception that some people belong to this informal, undefined group, and others are on the outside. Lewis calls this informal, undefined group "the inner ring." We find "the inner ring," claims Lewis, in every level of human society. He puts forward this thesis: "I believe that in all men's lives at certain periods . . . one of the most dominant elements is the desire to be inside the local Ring and the terror of being left outside."[1]

Lewis identified the "us and them" mentality that emerges in every level of society—the conviction that some of us are in some sense better than others and that this superior group should therefore make all the decisions and enjoy all the benefits.

Fundamentalism provides one of the clearest examples of the "us and them" mentality. Fundamentalism is a universal movement that cuts across every society, every religious group, and every nationality. Wherever it is found, fundamentalism can be identified by several "family resemblances." These family resemblances include

- developing a personal and communal identity around a set of religious ideals (that is, fundamentalists represent God).

- understanding truth to be revealed and unified and in their possession (that is, they have the truth).

- envisioning themselves on the positive side of a cosmic struggle (that is, they are the good guys).

- demonizing their opposition and consequently attempting to destroy them (that is, the bad guys need to be destroyed).[2]

At the heart of fundamentalism stands the "us and them" mentality to which C. S. Lewis points. Fundamentalism takes the subject a step further and says (and please excuse my misuse of grammar here) that since "us" are different from "them" and since "us" are better than "them," then "them" do not even have a right to exist. Us and them with a vengeance—that is the approach of fundamentalism.

Lest we think this is merely a modern-day phenomenon, all we have to do is turn to the New Testament. The "us and them" mentality appears often in the New Testament. We see it, for example, among the twelve disciples Jesus chooses to be the nucleus of the kingdom movement. When James and John secretly request that they be given the privileged positions at Jesus' right and left hand, they are attempting to establish an inner ring with them in it, distinguishing them from the other disciples (Matt 20:20-21).

We also see this mentality in the first church in Jerusalem when two groups, one identified as Hellenistic Jews and the other identified as Hebraic Jews, squabble over the distribution of the food. When the Hellenistic Jews complain that the Hebraic Jews receive privileged treatment, they are drawing an inner ring with themselves left out of it (Acts 6).

We find perhaps the clearest New Testament example of this "us and them" mentality in the church at Corinth, reflected in our text for this chapter. Paul identifies four clearly distinguished groups—Paul's group, Peter's group, Apollos's group, and a fourth group who called themselves followers of Jesus (v. 12). Each of these four groups tries to draw an inner ring with themselves in the privileged position. This "us and them" mentality, Paul declares, is destroying the fellowship of the church and deflects the church from its purpose.

Paul responds to these "us and them" divisions in the church at Corinth with three penetrating questions: *Is Christ divided? Was Paul crucified for you? Were you baptized into the name of Paul?* (v. 13). He assumes a negative answer to each of the questions. Jesus is not some spiritual prize to be parceled out among believers according to their own understanding. Jesus is a uniting force, not a source of division. No leader, however profound and powerful, can atone for our sins—only Jesus can do that. Furthermore, no individual, however spiritual and perceptive, can mark us as members of the family of God—only Jesus Christ can provide a firm foundation upon which to build our lives. *Is Christ divided? Was Paul crucified for you? Were you baptized into the name of Paul?* Paul asks (v. 13). And the answer to all three questions is "No."

The Corinthian Christians' confusion about those three crucial questions shatters their unity and diminishes their effectiveness for Christ, so Paul sends this word to them: *I appeal to you, brothers, in the name of our Lord Jesus Christ, that all of you agree with one another so that there may be no divisions among you and that you may be perfectly united in mind and thought* (v. 10). Paul wants no "us and them" in the Corinthian church.

Where does this mentality come from? It comes from the world. It comes from the culture of Corinth. In the paganism of the first-century world, a party spirit separates the rich from the poor and the master from the servant and the men from the women, and that spirit has invaded the church. In the paganism of the first-century world, political factions rally around high-profile figures, attacking those in other political parties. This kind of political maneuvering leaks over into the church. Paul declares that these things have no place in the church.

The first problem Paul deals with as he writes this letter to the Corinthian Christians is their tendency to allow the sociological patterns of the culture around them to infiltrate and influence the church.

We flirt with the same danger in our churches today. Sometimes a personality cult develops in the church around a certain pastor or staff member or teacher, either one who is serving at present or one who has served the church in the past. Instead of building the ministry on the foundation of Christ, we allow the ministry to become too closely identified with that personality. Sometimes we let the social stratification of the culture around us shape the way we relate to each other in the church, and we give in to these distinctions that Galatians 3:28 says should not be a part of the relationship matrix of the church. Sometimes political factions develop in the church around certain issues, whether it is the style of worship or some theological issue or a decision about ministry priorities, and the different political factions line up facing each other across the battlefield.

But here is the message of our text: Whenever we allow anyone other than Jesus to set the agenda for what we are doing, then we are not the church. Whenever we separate the rich from the poor or the men from the women or the Anglos from the ethnically diverse, excluding one group from leadership, then we are not the church. Whenever we divide into factions and bicker with each other instead of moving out in unity to touch the world with the gospel, then we are not the church. This "us and them" mentality is a part of pagan culture that we have allowed to infiltrate and influence the church. But the Bible is clear: there should be no "us and them" in the church.

What is the solution? Instead of different members of the church articulating different positions for the church, Paul urges the Corinthian Christians to *agree with one another* (v. 10). The Greek word here means to say the same thing or to speak with one voice. Paul wants them to be on the same page as they carry out their assignment in Corinth.

Instead of being divided into opposing groups, Paul wants them to *be perfectly united* (v. 10). The Greek word here is a surgical term for setting bones. We find the same word in Mark 1:19 where the author uses the term to describe the "mending" of the fishing nets so they can be effectively used. Paul wants the rips in the fabric of the church unity in Corinth to be mended so the people can effectively do the work God has called them to do.

Instead of having conflicting understandings of their approach as the people of God, Paul wants the Corinthians to be *united in mind* (v. 10). Paul refers here to our attitude or approach to life. Paul wants the Corinthian Christians to approach life with the mind of Christ instead of looking at things from their own perspectives.

Instead of different agendas that create dissention in the church, Paul wants the Corinthians to be *united in . . . thought* (v. 10). This word speaks of our intention or purpose. Paul wants the Corinthian Christians to focus on the same vision instead of seeking to promote their own agendas. Speaking with one voice, no divisions, united in understanding, and together in purpose—these phrases capture Paul's desire for the church at Corinth. These qualities must also characterize our churches today if we are to be what God has called us to be: united in speech, in thought, in purpose, and in action.

How can it happen? It can happen only in and through the transforming power of Jesus Christ. Notice that Paul begins our text with a reference to *the name of our Lord Jesus Christ* (v. 10), and he closes our text with a reference to *the cross of Christ* (v. 17). We cannot make it happen; only Jesus can.

How can people as diverse as the men and women who gather in the Corinthian church speak with one voice, avoid the party spirit, and be united in mind and thought? It can only happen through the transforming power of

Jesus Christ. How can people as diverse as the men and women who gather in our churches today speak with one voice, avoid the party spirit, and be united in mind and thought? The answer is the same: only through the transforming power of Jesus Christ. Only when we are marked by the name of Christ, motivated by the cross of Christ, and moved by the power of Christ can we shake free of the "us and them" mentality that creates inner rings that shut people out. Only then can we actually begin to experience the oneness that is ours in Christ Jesus. Only then can we really be the church. Here is the message in our text: there is no "us and them" in the church.

Note

1. C. S. Lewis, *The Weight of Glory* (New York: Simon & Schuster, 1975) 110–11.

The Message of the Church

1 Corinthians 1:18–25

Most of the writing about the church today deals with the question of how we can relate the gospel of Jesus to this post-modern, post-denominational, post-Christendom era in which we live. By "post-modern," I mean the growing suspicion of the concept of universal truth and the principles of modernism. By "post-denominational" I mean the sense of indifference to the name attached to any particular body of believers. By "post-Christendom" I mean the loss of the home-field advantage that came with the predominance of Christian thinking and principles that saturated and shaped American culture in the past. We live in a different world today, a world in which the exact meaning of "truth" is up for grabs, a world in which claiming to be a Baptist or Lutheran or Catholic is not as important as actually living like a Christian, and a world in which Christianity is only one of the teams playing in the spiritual arena of our world.

How do we communicate the gospel to this changing world? Church leaders today often talk about a "missional" strategy. That is, they remind us that we are all cross-cultural missionaries. Just as missionaries who go to a foreign land have to learn the language and customs of the people so they can relate the gospel to those who live there, we in our post-modern, post-denominational, post-Christendom world have to learn the language and the customs of the people of our day so that we can relate the gospel to them. This missional approach suggests that for people to accept the gospel, they must hear the message in "their heart language."

Popular writer Leonard Sweet describes this new spiritual context by referring to the different kinds of cups each member of his family prefers. His wife likes a cup with a handle so tiny he cannot even get his finger through it, he prefers a big mug, and his daughter prefers a Winnie-the-Pooh sippy cup. You can pour the same liquid into any of those cups, but the cups differ in size and shape. Sweet surmises that every generation has a cup that fits its own soul, and instead of making everyone drink out of the same cup, we need to find the cup they prefer and then pour the living water into it.[1]

As Paul plants the little group of Christians in the pluralistic, multicultural, urban, political, immoral city of Corinth, he also wants these Christians to be flexible about the containers into which they pour the gospel. After all, Paul is the one who says later in this same epistle, "I have become all things to all men so that by all possible means I might save some" (1 Cor 9:22). He reflects flexibility in his methods, but in the text for this chapter, Paul reminds the Corinthian Christians that they must be inflexible in their message. Paul affirms, *We preach Christ crucified* (v. 23). The church's message presents a Savior who died on the cross for the sins of the world and who calls us to a life of sacrificial service in his kingdom. That is the church's message, and that message must never change.

We need to recognize that many people in the world will not understand or accept this message. If the wisest thinkers of the world come together to determine how the world can be saved, they will never in a million years come up with the cross. The cross seems foolish to the world, not wise. If the most powerful leaders of the world come together to determine how to rescue the world, they will never develop the strategy of the cross. The cross seems like a defeat to the world, not a victory. Yet, according to our text, this gospel message about Jesus that centers on the cross is *to us who are being saved . . . the power of God* (v. 18). The irony of the gospel is that God brings deliverance through Jesus' apparent defeat and life through Jesus' death on the cross.

What does God accomplish for us through the cross? The New Testament writers search the conceptual encyclopedias of their day for metaphors to answer that question. From the law court they select the concept that Jesus is our advocate who brings a verdict of innocence from the omnipotent God who judges the world. From the slave market they solicit the idea that Jesus pays a ransom that sets us free. From the realm of personal relationships comes the suggestion that Jesus brings about reconciliation between us and God. From the temple they choose the image of Jesus offering himself as the sacrifice for our sin. From the battlefield they take the proposal that Jesus triumphs over the forces of evil. The New Testament writers draw metaphors from all realms of life to explain how Jesus' death on the cross affects us. All of these metaphors coalesce around this central truth: in the cross, Jesus fixes things between us and God and makes it possible for us to be reconciled to God.

God does not accomplish this redemptive work through some brilliantly executed maneuver or some irresistible power move. Instead, God accomplishes his redemptive work through the provisions and the persuasiveness of the cross. Paul wants the citizens of Corinth to remember that central truth as they attempt to contextualize the gospel in the culture of their first-century city.

How do the citizens of Corinth respond to the message of the cross? Actually, not very well. Notice how Paul describes their response.

To the Jews, Paul admits, the cross becomes *a stumbling block* (v. 23). Why? Apparently the Jews expect *miraculous signs* (v. 22). Having suffered under the burden of foreign oppression, the Jews look for manifestations of God's power. They want God to send down plagues on the enemies of his people as he did in the days of Moses. They want God to intercede with some act of dramatic power as he did during the Maccabean revolution. They want a manifestation of power. Instead, they get the cross, and the cross becomes a stumbling block to them.

To the Gentiles, Paul explains, the cross appears as *foolishness* (v. 23). Why? Apparently the Greeks look for wisdom. Influenced by their proverbial love of learning, the Greeks look for a reasonable account pleasingly presented to which they can give intellectual assent. They want a plan they can logically understand. They want a strategy their minds can grasp. Instead, they get the cross, and the cross appears to be foolishness to them. The Jews who want power reject the gospel because of its apparent weakness. The Greeks/Gentiles who want wisdom reject the gospel because of its apparent foolishness.

How does Paul respond to this resistance to the message of the cross? Will he water down the message to make it more compatible to his listeners? Will he adjust it to satisfy the expressed needs of his contemporaries? He will not. *Jews demand miraculous signs*, Paul asserts, *and Greeks look for wisdom, but we preach Christ crucified* (vv. 22-23).

The gospel draws a line in the sand and confronts every person with a decision. Will you have it the world's way or God's way? The gospel inevitably draws that line in the sand and calls for a decision. Will everyone understand the message? No. Will everyone like the message? No. Will everyone accept the message? No. But the message does not change: *Jews demand miraculous signs and Greeks look for wisdom, but we preach Christ crucified* (vv. 22-23, emphasis mine).

As we attempt to contextualize the gospel into the culture of the twenty-first century, we need to glean this lesson from our text. Our greatest challenge is not to get everyone to like our message or even to persuade everyone to accept our message. Our greatest challenge is to make sure we faithfully deliver the message because the cultural forces around us will constantly seek to dilute it.

Let me ask you a question. What is the most difficult thing a person can do? The old saying identifies two difficult accomplishments: to climb a fence that is leaning toward you and to kiss a girl who is leaning away from you. Both of those endeavors are difficult, but they are not the most difficult thing a person can do.

An older television commercial plays on this idea with a group of cowboys on horses bringing in a herd of cats. The commercial reminds us that anyone can bring in a herd of cattle, but herding cats is a different story. Herding cats is a difficult endeavor, but it is not the most difficult thing a person can do.

What is the most difficult thing a person can try to do? Make the gospel of Jesus Christ compatible with the culture. According to Webster, "compatible" means "in agreement with" or "congruent to." To make the gospel in agreement with or congruent to the culture is not merely difficult, it is impossible, for practically every value and virtue of modern culture clashes with the message of the gospel. We must make the gospel relevant to our culture, but we can never make it compatible. The world craves power to manipulate the lives of others and seeks wisdom to control the lives of others, but the message of the church in the twenty-first century is the same message Paul delivered to the Corinthians in the first century—a crucified Savior who calls us to a life of sacrificial service for the kingdom of God.

To be sure, we must present our message in a language that the world can understand so they can accept this message, be changed by it, and become a part of God's eternal kingdom, but we must never change the message. Like the Apostle Paul, we must continue to declare to the world, "We preach Christ crucified: a stumbling block to Jews and foolishness to Gentiles, but to those whom God has called, both Jews and Greeks, Christ the power of God and the wisdom of God." That is the message of the church, and it must never change.

Note

1. Leonard Sweet, *Aqua Church* (Loveland CO: Group Publishing, 1999) 29.

5

God Works in Mysterious Ways

1 Corinthians 1:26–31

Every time his foot pounds against the earth, the ground shakes and swirls of dust filter into the humid air of the Valley of Elah. The Philistine army lines up around him, but they are not crucial to the dramatic scene that day. They only fill in as scenery. The pivotal figure on that side of the valley is definitely the nine-foot giant named Goliath. Bronze covers his body from head to foot: a bronze helmet on his head, a bronze coat of armor protecting his massive chest, bronze shields around his legs, and a bronze javelin slung over his back The coat of armor alone weighs over 125 pounds. As Goliath strides defiantly back and forth at one end of the Valley of Elah, shouting his curses against Israel and daring anyone to come out and fight him, those on the other end of the valley literally shake in their sandals. Not one among them wants to face Goliath.

Saul can certainly confront Goliath, for Saul stands head and shoulders above the rest of his men and, after all, he is the God-anointed king of Israel. The most able of Saul's lieutenants can certainly take on Goliath, for they are trained for battle against the most overwhelming odds and, in addition, they have the promise of God's presence. But the Bible says, "On hearing the Philistine's words, Saul and all the Israelites were dismayed and terrified" (1 Sam 17:11). Not one among them dares to face Goliath. So the giant continues to stomp back and forth in front of the Philistine army, hurling threats and denigrating remarks at the people of God.

How will God win the victory over Goliath? We of course know the answer, but I want you to recognize that not one member of the army of Israel would have suggested David as the savior of Israel on that fateful day. Yet that is exactly what happened. The giant falls, plunging the Philistines into defeat, the Israelites emerge victorious, and God accomplishes this mighty feat through a little boy with no experience or training—a little boy who with his slingshot sinks a stone into the forehead of the giant.

How does David defeat the giant? David provides the answer in 1 Samuel 17:45: "You come against me with sword and spear and javelin, but I come against you in the name of the Lord Almighty." David does not really win the victory. God wins the victory through David.

The David and Goliath story provides a paradigm of how God advances his kingdom. He repeatedly uses the weakest and the least promising agents available to do his kingdom work. When God wants to deliver his people from Egyptian slavery, he chooses a stuttering murderer who suffers a self-imposed exile in the Arabian Desert. His name is Moses. When God wants someone on the inside to assist God's people in capturing the city of Jericho, he chooses a prostitute named Rahab. When God needs someone to establish the lineage that will produce the great king David and eventually the Messiah, he uses a foreigner from Moab named Ruth. When God wants a mother for the incarnate Son of God, he selects a young peasant girl named Mary from the insignificant village of Nazareth. God repeatedly uses the weakest and the least promising agents available to do his kingdom work.

What God did in biblical times he continues to do across the ages. In every crucial moment of the unfolding of God's kingdom, what Paul says in our text for this chapter is true: God has chosen *the foolish things of the world to shame the wise* and *the weak things of the world to shame the strong* (v. 27).

Not surprisingly, God employs the same strategy when he sends Paul to Corinth to contextualize the gospel in that pagan city. Paul identifies the people God uses in Corinth with three negative phrases in verse 26: *Not many of you were wise by human standards; not many were influential; not many were of noble birth*. "Wise" (*sophoi*) refers to the intellectual acuity of the Corinthian Christians. "Influential" (*dynatoi*) is the root of our word "dynamite" and describes those who have "clout" or "power" in society. "Of noble birth" (*eugeneis*) is the source of our word "genetics" and identifies their heritage or their bloodlines. "Not many of you," Paul reminds the Corinthians, are among the intellectually elite. "Not many of you" are influential in society. "Not many of you" are wellborn. Most of the men and women God uses to transform the city of Corinth appear foolish and weak in the eyes of the world.

Paul further describes these Corinthian Christians in verses 27-28 with four terms: foolish things, weak things, lowly things, and despised things. One commentator points out that Paul refers to them as "things" instead of "people" to indicate that, in the eyes of the world, these Corinthian Christians have so little value that they do not even count as individuals. In the eyes of the world, these Christians are nobodies. They are nothing, but with such as these, God builds his kingdom.

God chose the foolish things of the world to shame the wise; God chose the weak things of the world to shame the strong (v. 27). That is God's strategy for the Christians in Corinth: to contextualize the gospel into the pagan city of Corinth through people who seem to have so little to offer.

Why does God choose that strategy? Paul explains in verses 28-29: *He chose the lowly things of this world and the despised things—and the things that are not—to nullify the things that are, so that no one may boast before him.*

C. S. Lewis identifies pride as "the central vice," and he is probably right.[1] How quickly pride slips in the back door unnoticed, shaping words and inspiring actions that call the world's attention to ourselves instead of to God. And how often we exaggerate our own importance in the kingdom of God.

Dick Sheppard, a well-known Anglican preacher (1880–1937), was scheduled to deliver an important series of lectures. The night before the lectures, he developed a terrible cold that settled in his throat, and he was agitated about how this would affect his delivery the next day. Fussing and tossing on his bed, he finally fell asleep. He dreamed that he went to heaven and saw God pacing restlessly up and down. The Almighty was wringing his hands in despair and repeating, "What am I going to do? Dick Sheppard has a cold." Dick Sheppard awoke the next morning with a corrected view of his own importance.[2] We should awake each morning with that same realization. God can and will do very well without us, for the glory of the church and the power of the church is not us. It is God.

He chose the lowly things of this world and the despised things . . . so that no one may boast before him (vv. 28-29). We do not bring the victory. We do not further the kingdom. We do not transform the world. God does.

What does this mean for us today? Let me answer that question by identifying two possible sources for the idea Paul presents in our text and for the quote with which the passage ends in verse 31: *Let him who boasts boast in the Lord.* What is Paul's source?

The usual answer is that Paul quotes the prophet Jeremiah here, and most of our translations of the New Testament have a marginal note referencing Jeremiah 9:24. In Jeremiah 9, the prophet issues a word of judgment to the people of Israel. At the beginning of that chapter, the prophet calls Israel "a crowd of unfaithful people" (9:2). At the end of the chapter, he pronounces this word of judgment: "The days are coming, declares the LORD, when I will punish all who are circumcised in the flesh," and then he concludes, "And even the whole house of Israel is uncircumcised in heart" (9:25, 26). In the midst of that message of judgment, the prophet proclaims, "Let him who boasts boast about this: that he understands and knows me" (9:24).

If that is Paul's source, then he probably intends this word to the Corinthians to be a word of judgment, to them and to us. When we become puffed up with our own importance and forget that we are what we are and we accomplish what we accomplish only through God's power, then we will have to answer to God for our pride. This can be a word of judgment for us today.

However, some scholars identify a different source. Some believe that Paul's reference is the prayer of Hannah in 1 Samuel 2:1-10. In 1 Samuel 2, Hannah praises God for using someone as insignificant as she to accomplish his kingdom work. "My heart rejoices in the LORD, in the LORD my horn is lifted high," she prays (2:1). Then she adds, "He raises the poor from the dust and lifts the needy from the ash heap; he seats them with princes and has them inherit a throne of honor" (2:8). Why do some scholars think Paul has in mind this passage in 1 Samuel 2 when he sends this word to the Corinthian Christians? In the Greek version of the Old Testament, the Septuagint or LXX, Hannah's prayer has a long conclusion that is lacking in the Hebrew text of 1 Samuel 2:1-10. There, her prayer ends with these words: "Do not let the wise man boast in his understanding, and do not let the powerful man boast in his power, and do not let the wealthy man boast in his wealth. But let the one who boasts boast in this, to understand and know the *Lord* and to do justice and righteousness in the midst of the earth" (1 Kingdoms 2:10, LXX).

If that is Paul's source, then he probably intends this word to the Corinthians to be a word of encouragement, to them and to us. When we become overwhelmed with our incompetence and our inconsistency and our nothingness, and we are ready to give up, we need to remember that God specializes in using people just like us to advance his kingdom. This can be a word of encouragement for us.

I think this final verse in our text should be for us *both* a word of judgment and a word of encouragement, a word of judgment that reminds us we can be too big for God to use, and a word of encouragement that reminds us we can never be too small for God to use.

God sends the first Christians out into the pagan city with the message of a Savior who dies on the cross for the sins of the world and who calls us to a life of sacrificial service in his kingdom, and he uses nobodies to do the job. This bunch of nobodies with the message of the cross transforms the city. The poet William Cowper was right: "God moves in a mysterious way His wonders to perform."[3]

Notes

1. C. S. Lewis, *Mere Christianity* (New York: Simon & Schuster, 1943) 109.

2. Leslie B. Flynn, *Serve Him with Joy* (Wheaton IL: Key Publishers, 1960) 49.

3. *The Oxford Dictionary of Quotations* (London: Oxford University Press, 1941) 161.

6

Jesus Christ and Him Crucified

1 Corinthians 2:1-5

In 1996, Baylor University sponsored a search for the most effective preachers in the English-speaking world. This effort, led by Dr. Larry Lyon, produced a list of twelve men and women whom they touted as the most effective preachers of our day.

From a slightly different approach and with a slightly different method of selection, Michael Duduit, editor of *Preaching* magazine, came up with a list of the "Ten Greatest Preachers of the Twentieth Century."[1] Billy Graham was the only repeat from the Baylor list. The greatest preacher in the twentieth century, according to *Preaching* magazine, was James Stewart, the gifted Scottish preacher who served at one time as the chaplain to the Queen of Scotland.

The most effective communicator of the gospel in all of Christian history is noticeably missing from both lists, which is okay because he would not have wanted to be on such a list. In fact, he would have been embarrassed to have appeared on such a list. I know that because of what he writes to the Corinthian Christians in our text for this chapter. He writes these words:

> When I came to you, brothers, I did not come with eloquence or superior wisdom as I proclaimed to you the testimony about God. For I resolved to know nothing while I was with you except Jesus Christ and him crucified. I came to you in weakness and fear, and with much trembling. My message and my preaching were not with wise and persuasive words, but with a demonstration of the Spirit's power, so that your faith might not rest on men's wisdom, but on God's power. (vv. 1-5)

Paul declares that he does not come to Corinth with either "eloquence" or "superior wisdom," nor does he preach with "wise and persuasive words." What does that mean? We can look at each of these words individually, but I think it will be more instructive to grasp the big picture. "Eloquence" and "superior wisdom" and "wise and persuasive words" form the foundation for the rhetorical scheme of his day. The study of rhetoric, which Webster defines as "the art of using words effectively in speaking or writing," began in Greece in the fifth century BC. Democratic government emerges in Athens, and in some of the other cities of ancient Greece, based on the assumption that all citizens have an equal right to participate in their own government. To do so, however, they have to be able to speak in public, for decisions are made in assemblies composed of adult male citizens, and those who can most persuasively present their ideas dominate these debates.

Some people, of course, seem to have a natural gift for communication. Others develop those skills by attaching themselves to teachers called "sophists" who teach their students how to be effective in public life by marshaling arguments, by dividing speeches into logical parts, and by carefully choosing and combining words. Socrates distrusted the teaching of the sophists, suggesting that rhetoric is nothing more than a form of flattery, morally irresponsible and not based on knowledge of the truth. Aristotle, on the other hand, suggested that rhetoric is morally neutral. That is, it can be manipulative and irresponsible, or it can be used for good. The persuasiveness of our speech, according to Aristotle, depends on three things: the logical validity of what is being argued, the generation of trust in the audience toward the speaker, and the emotional stirring that motivates the audience to accept the views advanced and act in accordance with them. Or, as Aristotle's theory came to be expressed, the effectiveness of our speech is determined by *logos, ethos,* and *pathos.*[2]

Five centuries later, these rhetorical practices still influenced the culture in cities such as first-century Corinth. When Paul arrives in Corinth to preach the gospel, he claims that he does not come to them with "eloquence" and "superior wisdom" and "wise and persuasive words," he simply affirms that he does not rely on rhetorical technique. He does not use deceptive methods to manipulate the crowd into an easy acceptance of the gospel. He does not carefully choose and combine words because of the effect they may have on the audience. He does not depend on *logos, ethos,* and *pathos* to maneuver men and women into the kingdom. He simply presents the message of the gospel and depends on the Spirit of God to bring conviction and conversion.

My message and my preaching were not with wise and persuasive words, he explains to the Corinthian Christians, *but with a demonstration of the Spirit's power, so that your faith might not rest on men's wisdom, but on God's power* (vv. 4-5). He does not depend on rhetoric. Instead, he depends on the efficacy of the message and on the power of the Holy Spirit.

This is probably a good place to insert a parenthesis and deal with an issue I might have raised by this discussion and by the thrust of the last two chapters. Paul's emphasis in the opening of 1 Corinthians on the message and not the messenger (1:18-25), on the insignificant instruments God uses to communicate that message (1:26-31), and on the simple method Paul uses to proclaim that message (2:1-5) can lead to confusion about our part in contextualizing the gospel in our culture. Paul does not say that our part in the process is not important, nor does Paul suggest that we can settle for shabbiness or half-heartedness or mediocrity in our Christian lives. The one who calls the Corinthians at the end of chapter 12 of this letter to "the most excellent way" (12:31) will never be satisfied with shabbiness. The one who tells the Corinthians later in this same letter, "I beat my body and make it my slave so that after I have preached to others, I myself will not be disqualified for the prize" (9:27), will never accept half-heartedness. And the one who later tells the Corinthians, "So whether you eat or drink or whatever you do, do it all for the glory of God" (10:31), will never settle for mediocrity.

Paul does not suggest that we settle for shabbiness or half-heartedness or mediocrity in our Christian lives. Anyone who uses this passage to justify just doing enough to get by or doing the Lord's work in our own weak way totally misunderstands Paul's point. We must always strive for excellence in kingdom work, we must always give one hundred and ten percent as Christians, and we must always do our best. Shabbiness and half-heartedness and mediocrity are never acceptable in the life of a Christian or in the work of the church.

In his memoir *On Writing*, Stephen King describes the proper approach of a writer to his assignment. He concludes, "You can approach the act of writing with nervousness, excitement, hopefulness, or even despair—the sense that you can never completely put on the page what's in your mind and heart. You can come to the act with your fists clenched and your eyes narrowed . . . . You can come to it because you want a girl to marry you or because you want to change the world. Come to it any way but lightly. Let me say it again: *you must not come lightly to the blank page.*"[3]

Paul echoes that sentiment on more than one occasion. He agrees that we cannot and should not come lightly to the work of the kingdom. Doing

God's kingdom work demands nothing less than our best effort every day of our lives in everything we do for Christ. Yet Paul's point remains: the effectiveness of our efforts is not in the excellence of our presentation; it is in the efficacy of the message.

What is this message that has the power to transform a pagan city? Paul tells us in verse 2: *For I resolved to know nothing while I was with you except Jesus Christ and him crucified.*

Paul's message is, first of all, a message about "Jesus Christ." Jesus is the central focus of Paul's message and should also be for us today. Why should Jesus be the central focus of our message? Paul elevates Jesus as the one who provides salvation for us. In the words of the first-century preacher, Peter, "Salvation is found in no one else, for there is no other name under heaven given to men by which we must be saved" (Acts 4:12).

Some modern commentators have discerned in the Bible three different types of stories that identify the human condition: human beings as sinners who need to be forgiven; human beings in bondage who need to be liberated; and human beings in exile who need to be brought back home. Whichever metaphor we prefer, the point of the gospel message is the same: only Jesus can provide what we need. Only Jesus can forgive us, and only Jesus can liberate us, and only Jesus can bring us back home to the Father. Jesus is the one who provides salvation for us. That is why, when Paul goes to the city of Corinth, he preaches about Jesus Christ. That is also why we should make Jesus central in our message today.

Paul's message also focuses on the cross. He preaches, "Jesus Christ and him crucified." The cross stands at the center of Paul's message, and should also be the center for us today. Why should the cross be the central focus of our message? Paul believes that the cross is God's instrument for our salvation. In his letter to the Colossian Christians, Paul expresses this idea in these terms: "For God was pleased . . . through him to reconcile to himself all things, whether things on earth or things in heaven, by making peace through his blood, shed on the cross" (Col 1:19-20). On the cross, Jesus pays the price for our sin so we can be forgiven. On the cross, Jesus defeats the prince of darkness so we can be liberated. On the cross, Jesus removes the barrier erected by our sin so we can be reconciled to God.

That is why, when Paul goes to the city of Corinth, he preaches about the cross. That is also why we should make the cross central in our message today. Jesus Christ and him crucified—that is Paul's message when he tries to contextualize the gospel in the first-century city of Corinth. It must also be our message today.

Notes

1. For the article identifying all ten of these top preachers, go to www.preaching.com/resources/articles/11565635.

2. Aristotle, *On Rhetoric*, trans. George A. Kennedy (New York: Oxford University Press, 1991) vii–x.

3. Stephen King, *On Writing* (New York: Scribner, 2000) 106.

7

The Wisdom of Christ

1 Corinthians 2:6–16

As they examine church members in America today, many observers suggest that they can find little difference between those who claim to be followers of Jesus Christ and those who do not, between those who are in the church and those who are outside the church. When Christians do rise up to distinguish themselves from the world, they often take the negative approach of identifying all the things they are against and vehemently condemning those who are guilty of these things.

In contrast to that approach, we recognize that the first Christians turn the world upside down not because of what they are *against* but because of what they are *for*. A new perception drives these first Christians, and a new purpose permeates their lives with a passion that the world simply cannot resist. Positive commitments and not negative restrictions distinguish the first-century church.

Exactly how does that perception and purpose and passion work itself out in the first-century church? We cannot easily answer that question because of the diversity of churches in the New Testament. We often mistakenly refer to "the New Testament church" as if it is a singular entity with a homogenous character. Actually, we can identify a number of churches in the New Testament, and these churches differ as much as churches today.

A depth of fellowship in which people provide care and support for everyone characterizes the Jerusalem church (Acts 2). A world mission vision shapes the Antioch church (Acts 11, 13). The Berean church focuses more on the study of God's word (Acts 17). A dull mediocrity marks the Laodicean church, causing the risen Christ to say, "Because you are lukewarm—neither hot nor cold—I am about to spit you out of my mouth" (Rev 3:16). The Corinthian church continually struggles to keep the value system of the world out of the church. As a result, the Corinthian church often disintegrates into divisions. At times, the immorality of church members stuns the church leaders. Self-centeredness often mars the church's fellowship and keeps it from truly ministering to all of the members. While acknowledging that the Corinthian church differs from the other New Testament churches, we have to admit that it seems to be more like our churches today.

That is why I have chosen to focus on the Corinthian church as we examine our challenge to contextualize the gospel in our communities. The Corinthian church makes many of the same mistakes we make today, and no other book in the New Testament so honestly explores those mistakes as does Paul's first letter to the church at Corinth.

Paul addresses this letter "to the church of God in Corinth, to those sanctified in Christ Jesus" (1:2). In other words, these Christians in Corinth are set apart to be distinct from those in Corinth who do not follow Christ. But what distinguishing marks are to set them apart from their fellow citizens? In our text for this chapter, Paul gives us the answer. Jesus has given these Corinthians a new perception of what life is about. Notice how Paul develops this thought in the opening verses of our text.

Earlier Paul tells the Corinthians that he does not come to them "with wise and persuasive words" (2:4), but now, in verse 6, Paul declares, *We do, however, speak a message of wisdom among the mature.* Has Paul changed his mind? No. In verse 6, Paul talks about a different kind of wisdom and speaks to a different audience. In the previous passage, Paul has in mind the wisdom of the world. "Wisdom" in 2:6-16 refers to the secret wisdom that comes from God. In the previous passage, Paul's audience is the world. In the current text, the audience is the church. In the world, Paul does not speak the world's wisdom. However, in the church, Paul explains, he does talk about wisdom, but it is the secret wisdom from God.

What is this secret wisdom from God? What is this new perception given to Paul and to the Corinthian Christians? Paul identifies this wisdom earlier in 1 Corinthians 1:23-24. This special wisdom revolves around the cross. God reveals that he will save the world through Jesus' death on the cross and his ultimate resurrection. Consequently, Christians understand that the defining event in human history—the event around which all human history revolves—is the life, death, and resurrection of Jesus Christ. That is what sets these Christians in Corinth apart from their fellow citizens. They have a new perception of what life is about.

Where does that perception come from? Paul makes it clear that we do not gain it by using our human faculties. The new perception comes from God. Paul makes this point in verse 9 with what seems to be a paraphrase of a passage in Isaiah 64:3: *No eye has seen, no ear has heard, no mind has conceived what God has prepared for those who love him.* In this familiar statement, Paul does not focus on what we will experience someday in heaven, which is how we usually interpret this passage. Instead, he has in mind the spiritual truth we can discern here and now.

We do not grasp this secret wisdom by the use of our "eye"—through our normal method of perceiving what is going on around us. We do not grasp this special perception by the use of our "ear"—through the knowledge passed from one generation to the next. We do not grasp this special perception by the use of our "mind"—through the use of insight to perceive truth. Our normal cognitive perception, the tradition passed down to us, and the use of intuition may help us understand human opinions, but it is all worthless in fathoming the secret wisdom of God.

How can we grasp this special perception about life? How can we be convinced that God's plan is to save the world through Jesus' death on the cross? Paul affirms that God has to reveal this truth to us. '*No eye has seen, no ear has heard, no mind has conceived what God has prepared for those who love him*'—*but God has revealed it to us by his Spirit* (vv. 9-10). We grasp this special perception about life because the Holy Spirit who is at work within us reveals the truth to us.

Do you remember what Jesus says about the Holy Spirit on the final night of his life? To his disciples gathered around him, Jesus promises, "I will ask the Father, and he will give you another Counselor to be with you forever—the Spirit of truth" (John 14:16-17). Then, at Pentecost, the Holy Spirit fulfills this promise by coming to the first disciples. But the Holy Spirit is not just for the disciples. Peter promises the Spirit to everyone who believes. In his Pentecost sermon, he declares to the crowd listening to him preach, "Repent and be baptized, every one of you, in the name of Jesus Christ for the forgiveness of your sins. And you will receive the gift of the Holy Spirit" (Acts 2:38).

The Corinthian Christians also receive the Holy Spirit. *We have not received the spirit of the world but the Spirit who is from God,* Paul reminds them in verse 14. The Spirit of God reveals to the Christians at Corinth this special perception about life: the life, death, and resurrection of Jesus Christ formed the defining moment in human history.

The wisdom of God revealed by the Spirit of God that provides the child of God a new perception of the purpose of God—that is the truth Paul presents in our text. But then Paul takes the subject a step further.

This new perception instills us as Christians with a new purpose. Or, to put it another way, this new understanding of what life is about motivates us to live in a different way. Paul captures this idea in the final verse of our text. As a result of this secret wisdom of God that has been revealed to us through his Spirit, Paul concludes, *We have the mind of Christ* (v. 16).

What does Paul mean when he claims that we have the "mind of Christ"? Perhaps the clue to understanding the use of the phrase "the mind of Christ" is in Paul's use of that phrase in Philippians 2:5. The King James Version translates it like this: "Let this mind be in you, which was also in Christ Jesus." Then Paul goes on to explain what the mind of Christ is: "Who, being in very nature God, did not consider equality with God something to be grasped, but made himself nothing, taking the very nature of a servant, being made in human likeness. And being found in appearance as a man, he humbled himself and became obedient to death—even death on a cross!" (Phil 2:5-8). To have the mind of Christ means to be driven by the same purpose that motivates Jesus Christ himself, to live a life of humility and helpfulness like he does, and to be willing to take up our cross and follow him. It means to have a passion for the things of God.

This conclusion brings us back to where I began the chapter. The first Christians turn the world upside down not because of what they are against but because of what they are for. A new perception and a new purpose permeate the lives of these first-century Christians with a new passion that the world simply cannot resist. That new perception, purpose, and passion come to these first-century disciples when the Spirit of God transforms their lives.

What does this mean for us today? It reminds us that our future effectiveness as a church does not depend on our wisdom, our giftedness, our power, or our strategic planning. It depends on our willingness right now, every day, in everything we do as a church to be informed and transformed by the Spirit of God.

John Hyde, the son of a Presbyterian minister, grew up in Illinois, but when he finished seminary training at McCormick Seminary in Chicago, he left for India where for two decades he made a significant contribution to the kingdom through his preaching and especially through his praying. Perhaps the secret of his impact is found in an experience that happened to him on his first voyage to India.

As he boarded the ship to head for India that first time, someone handed him a telegram. He hurriedly opened it on the deck of the ship. The only words in the telegram were, "John Hyde, are you filled with the Spirit of God?" The telegram made him mad. He crumpled it and pushed it down in his pocket. When he was finally settled in his cabin, he went to bed, but he could not sleep. He tossed and turned. In the early morning hours, he got out of bed, found the telegram, and read it again: "John Hyde, are you filled with the Spirit of God?" He thought to himself, "The audacity of someone asking me that question! I have given my life to the Lord. I have prepared myself in seminary. And here I am a missionary, sincere, dedicated, leaving my home, going to another country. How dare someone ask if I am filled with the Spirit of God?" But then another reading of the telegram convicted his heart, and he fell down on his knees and cried out to God, "O, God, the audacity of me to think that I could pray or preach or witness or live or serve or do anything in my own strength and in my own power. Give me your strength, God. Fill me with your Spirit." With the Spirit of God in control of his life, John Hyde was captured by a perception and driven by a purpose that permeated his life with a passion the world could not resist.[1]

Dare we ask ourselves that same question? The answer will determine whether or not we become a transformed people who transform the world, for the Spirit is the source of the perception, the purpose, and the passion we must have to touch our communities for Christ. *Are you filled with the Spirit of God?*

Note

1. Daniel Vestal, "Triumphant Living," sermon preached at the First Baptist Church, Midland TX, 5 July 1981.

8

Worldly Christians Versus Spiritual Christians

1 Corinthians 3:1-9

This letter we know as 1 Corinthians is Paul's response to a report he received concerning the church in Corinth from some members of Chloe's household (1:11). Hearing this report, Paul realizes things are not exactly right in the church at Corinth. The Christians at Corinth are not "being transformed into his [Christ's] likeness with ever-increasing glory" (2 Cor 3:18), nor are they transforming the city. Something seems to be wrong.

A casual reading of our text for today might lead us to locate the church's problem in the divisions that pit the members against each other in intramural squabbles. To be sure, jealousy and quarreling do exist among the Corinthian Christians. Some members of the church line up behind Paul, and others line up behind Apollos (3:4). Divisions do exist in the church at Corinth. However, these divisions are not the problem; they are the symptoms of the problem. The problem runs deeper than the rifts in their fellowship. The Corinthians have a spiritual problem. Instead of being "spiritual," they are "worldly." *I could not address you as spiritual*, Paul says in verse 1 of our text, *but as worldly.*

What do these words mean—spiritual and worldly? Paul explains in our text for this chapter.

In verses 3-4, Paul illustrates what it means to be worldly. In the first-century world of Corinth, teachers known as "sophists" hold key positions in society, not only speaking at public performances but also running expensive schools where they train the next generation of sophists. The sophists call the students enrolled in their exclusive schools their *disciples*. Intense competition exists between these sophists who seek the acclaim of the public. These teachers—or more often their disciples—frequently get into shouting matches in the public square, arguing about which teacher is more brilliant and ridiculing the other teacher for his weaknesses.

Pundits of the day describe the chaos created by the competitiveness of these contending disciples as *eris*, a word that means *strife*. They also describe the relationship between the disciple and his teacher in the city of Corinth with the word *zelos,* which means *zeal.* This term describes the zealousness with which the disciples promote and defend their teacher before the disciples of other teachers. *Eris* and *zelos,* jealousy and quarreling—those words describe the Corinthian culture of that day.[1]

In verse 3, Paul uses those exact words to describe the Corinthian Christians: *For since there is jealousy* [zelos] *and quarreling* [eris] *among you, are you not worldly?* Paul calls the Christians in Corinth "worldly" because they act just like the people in the world. They appear to believe that the purpose of life is to build up their own kingdom instead of building up the kingdom of God. They act like the goal in life is to draw attention to themselves instead of drawing people to God. They imply that the work of the church is about them instead of about God. They see things from the perspective of the world. Paul writes to them, *I could not address you as spiritual but as worldly* (v. 1).

In verses 5-8, Paul illustrates what it means to be spiritual. *What, after all, is Apollos?* he writes in verse 5. *And what is Paul? Only servants, through whom you came to believe—as the Lord has assigned to each his task.* The word translated "servants" can be literally translated "field hand." The Christians in Corinth who argue about which one is the greatest, Paul or Apollos, and who attribute to themselves spiritual stature because of their exalted spiritual knowledge, completely miss the point. They are just field hands in God's harvest doing what God has assigned them to do.

That is what Paul means with the term "spiritual." To be spiritual means to understand that the goal in life is not to draw attention to us but to draw attention to God. To be spiritual means to understand that everything good that happens is because of God's power, not ours. To be spiritual means to realize that the work of the church is not about us. It is about God. Because he does not see those traits displayed in their lives, Paul announces to the Corinthians, *I could not address you as spiritual but as worldly* (v. 1).

Reading this letter from Paul probably shocks the Corinthians because they think of themselves as being mature, not as infants. They consider themselves to be spiritual, not worldly. Yet, by the attention they draw to themselves, their pride in themselves, their focus on themselves, and their concern about themselves, these Christian leaders in Corinth demonstrate that they are not spiritual at all. To be spiritual simply means to understand that we are just field hands in God's harvest doing what God has assigned us to do.

English preacher F. B. Meyer served as pastor of a church located in the shadow of two other great churches, one where Charles Spurgeon was the pastor and the other where G. Campbell Morgan was the pastor. Meyer explained his relationship to these two other churches in one of his sermons. He said,

> I find in my own ministry that supposing I pray for my own little flock, God bless me, God fill my pews, God send me a revival, I miss the blessing, but as I pray for my big brother, Mr. Spurgeon, on the right-hand side of my church, God bless him; or my other big brother Campbell Morgan, on the other side of my church, God bless him, I am sure to get a blessing without praying for it, for the overflow of their cups fills my little bucket.

The work of the kingdom is not about us. It is about God.

Few have made an impact for Christ like a diminutive Catholic nun from Albania who came to be known as Mother Teresa. For decades she led a work centered in the worst area of Calcutta that eventually affected the entire world. When people gave her accolades, this woman whose name became a household word in the world, who won the Nobel Peace Prize, whose Missionaries of Charity became the hand of God throughout the world would always shrug them off by saying, "I am an instrument, a little pencil in the hands of the Lord. Nothing more than that."[3] The work of the kingdom is not about us. It is about God.

In the middle of the eighteenth century, Christians in England did to John Wesley and George Whitefield what the Corinthian Christians did to Paul and Apollos. Some lined up behind John Wesley as their spiritual leader and some lined up behind George Whitefield, creating a rivalry between the two. The followers of John Wesley even began calling themselves Wesleyans. Some of George's followers asked him if they should call themselves Whitefieldians. "No," George Whitefield wrote in spring 1749, "let the name of Whitefield die so that the cause of Jesus Christ may live."[4] The work of the kingdom is not about us. It is about God.

These illustrations from history demonstrate the goal to which Paul points the Corinthian Christians when he writes, *I could not address you as spiritual but as worldly* (v. 1). Paul calls them worldly because they have the same perspective, are driven by the same passions, and live according to the same priorities as those in the world.

Where do you think Paul gets that understanding of spirituality? He gets it from Jesus. Do you remember the scene painted in Luke 22 in the last days of Jesus' ministry, with the shadow of the cross already falling across his life, his face resolutely set to go to Jerusalem? Trailing behind him are the twelve, these whom Jesus has individually called and specifically trained. For three years he poured his life into theirs. Now the purpose for which he came to the earth looms large before him. The shadow of the cross has fallen across his life. In facing the cross he will fulfill God's plan and establish God's kingdom. Do you remember what the disciples argue about on the way to Jerusalem? They argue about which of them will be the greatest, about what great honor will come to them when Jesus establishes his kingdom. Later, as they gather around the table for the last supper together, Jesus reprimands the disciples for their distorted perspective and gives them this word of instruction: "The kings of the Gentiles lord it over them; and those who exercise authority over them call themselves Benefactors. But you are not to be like that. Instead, the greatest among you should be like the youngest, and the one who rules like the one who serves" (Luke 22:25-26). The work of the kingdom is not about us; it is about God.

In one of the churches where I served as pastor, a church member approached me one day with a desire to serve God's kingdom. He told me, "Preacher, treat me like a checker. Just move me wherever you need me to be." That modern-day disciple captures the spirit of Paul's call to the Corinthian Christians to be spiritual instead of worldly.

Notes

1. Bruce W. Winter, *After Paul Left Corinth: The Influence of Secular Ethics and Social Change* (Grand Rapids MI: William B. Eerdmans, 2001) 39.

2. W. Y. Fullerton, *No Ordinary Man: The Remarkable Life of F. B. Meyer* (Belfast: Ambassador Productions, 1993) 132.

3. Navin Chawla, *Mother Teresa: The Authorized Biography* (Rockport MA: Element, 1992) 195.

4. John Pollock, *George Whitefield and the Great Awakening* (Garden City NY: Doubleday & Company, 1972) 239.

9

The Foundation of the Church

1 Corinthians 3:10-17

I confess that over the years I have misinterpreted this passage. I have always interpreted it as a statement about individual believers. As individual believers, our lives are built upon the foundation of Christ, and we have to decide what kind of life we will build on that foundation. Someday we will have to give an account to God for the kind of life we have built. Some individuals build with good material and will be blessed in heaven. Others build with bad material and will still get into heaven, but just barely. I have interpreted this passage as a description of the individual believer.

However, as I have studied this passage again recently, I realize that this is not a passage about individual believers. Instead, it is about the church. The text does not describe what happens to individual believers when they face judgment. Instead, it describes what happens when we do not build the church on the right foundation and with the right materials. This passage is a description of the church.

How do we build the church? We must begin with the foundation. What is the right foundation for the church? Paul declares, *For no one can lay any foundation other than the one already laid, which is Jesus Christ* (v. 11). In his Ephesian letter, Paul changes the imagery slightly and calls Jesus "the chief cornerstone" (2:20) Then he concludes, "In him the whole building is joined together and rises to become a holy temple in the Lord" (2:20). Both passages make the same point. We must build the church on the right foundation, and that foundation is Jesus Christ.

Yet even when the foundation is secure, that is not enough, for the Bible says God has given us the responsibility to build upon that foundation. We have to choose what material we will use to build. Paul explains to the Corinthians, *If any man builds on this foundation using gold, silver, costly stones, wood, hay, or straw, his work will be shown for what it is* (v. 12).

Paul does not present these six elements as code words for some deeper truth. He simply says that some build the church with perishable, combustible materials that will not stand the test of time. Others build the church with imperishable, indestructible materials that will last. He challenges the Corinthians to build the church with the kind of building material that will last.

Why is it important to build the church on the right foundation and with the right building material? A testing time will come: *His work will be shown for what it is, because the Day will bring it to light* (v. 13). Paul might be using "the Day" as a general reference to the passing of time. In that case, Paul simply says our work will be tested by the passing of time. However, most commentators agree that with this term "the Day," Paul does not refer simply to the passing time but specifically to the end time. In other words, Paul refers to the Day of the Lord when God's ultimate judgment will be manifest. (We see similar references in Rom 2:5; 1 Cor 1:8; 2 Cor 1:14; and 1 Thess 5:2). Notice, however, in this case that the purpose of this ultimate judgment is not to punish the church (Jude 7; Rev 18:8), to destroy the church (Matt 3:10; Heb 10:27), or even to refine the church (Zech 13:9; 1 Pet 1:7) but to disclose the quality of the church we have built.

Paul takes the subject a step further in verses 14-15 with the reminder that this time of testing will result in either rewards or rebuke. He writes, *If what he has built survives, he will receive his reward. If it is burned up, he will suffer loss; he himself will be saved, but only as one escaping through the flames* (vv. 14-15). If we do not build God's church on the right foundation with the right material, dire consequences will come to us.

Paul adds an even more chilling note in verses 16-17. If we do not build God's church on the right foundation with the right material, dire consequences will also come to God's church. We do not represent only ourselves as Christians; we represent God. We are not merely dealing with another human organization; we are dealing with God's church. That is why Paul adds this note of warning: *If anyone destroys God's temple, God will destroy him; for God's temple is sacred, and you are that temple* (v. 17). This verse describes the Spirit indwelling the gathered community of God's people, and Paul's point is clear: if the church is the dwelling place of God, then God will deal severely with those who corrupt it or damage it.

Let me summarize the message of our text. We are responsible to build the church on the foundation of Jesus Christ. We can build the church with perishable material that does not last or with imperishable material that endures. In the passing of time and in the end time, our work will be tested and the kind of church we have built will be revealed. Failure to build a church that lasts will result in dire consequences in our lives. God's church will also suffer from our shoddy workmanship. Therefore, building the church is serious business. That is true of the first-century church. It is also true of the church in the twenty-first century.

How can we do it? How can we build a church on the foundation of Jesus Christ that endures and brings glory to God? I will offer provisional answers to that question.

Building the church begins with *prayer*. If we are to build a church on the foundation of Jesus Christ, then we must do what Jesus tells us to do, and Jesus repeatedly calls us to pray. Do you remember Jesus' reflection on the world in Matthew 9? As Jesus travels around the countryside, the crowds press against him. Jesus describes them as being "harassed and helpless, like sheep without a shepherd" (9:36). Then he turns to his disciples and says, "The harvest is plentiful but the workers are few. Ask the Lord of the harvest, therefore, to send out workers into his harvest field" (9:37-38). Before we can go and tell others about Jesus, we must pray. Before we can build the church, we must pray. Before we can transform the world with the truth of the gospel, we must pray. Before we can do anything, we must pray. Jesus tells his disciples to pray for the harvest.

I heard a sermon several years ago from Rick Davis, who worked with the Center for Evangelism in the Baptist General Convention of Texas. He told of preaching in a church several miles outside San Antonio. It was just a small church in a small town. He said the church had baptized eight people the previous year. He used this passage from Matthew 9 and told the church that what Jesus wanted them to do, more than anything else, was to pray for the harvest. The next Sunday, instead of having a sermon, the pastor gathered his people around him, and they spent the entire hour from 11:00 to 12:00 just praying for the harvest, asking that God would use them to win the people of their community to Jesus Christ. The next day, a single mom from the community stopped by the church to see the pastor. She did not go to his church nor was she a Christian. Yet she told the pastor that she had an impression that she needed to come by the church and talk to him. She said that impression began to build in her the previous morning, Sunday, at about 11:30. The pastor talked to her about Jesus, and she made a commitment of her life. He went home with her and shared Christ with her two daughters, and they made a commitment to Christ as well. The next Sunday he baptized those three, nearly half as many in one Sunday as he had baptized the entire previous year. The pastor was convinced that this remarkable turnaround occurred primarily because his church decided to take Jesus seriously when he told us to pray for the harvest.

If we are going to build the church on the foundation of Jesus Christ, then we must do what he told us to do. We must pray for the harvest. We must pray that we can become a transformed church that transforms the world. We must pray.

Then we must *infiltrate the community*. If we are going to build the church on the foundation of Jesus Christ, then we must be what he told us to be—the salt and light that permeates the community and transforms it (Matt 5:13-16). We have to quit worrying that the world will influence us and begin influencing the world. We have to realize that we are most effectively being the church not inside the church building but outside it.

I heard William Hinson, gifted Methodist minister, recount the story of his appointment to a church in a large city that had lost almost a thousand members from its best days. When he took his assignment, he knew he would have to do something drastic, so he asked all who were willing to leave their easy chairs and televisions to come meet him the following night to do visitation evangelism. Only a handful came, among them a retired missionary named Rhoda Burdeshaw. She was in her seventies then, suffered from severe arthritis, drove an old green Oldsmobile that did not have six square inches of undented areas on it, and had in her hand one of the old-time flashlights about two feet long, with six batteries turned end to end. When she asked the pastor for some cards, he hesitated to give her any because he was afraid she could not see the street signs and might get hurt in the rather rough neighborhood around the church. He wanted her to go with someone. She protested, "Preacher, we don't have enough people here to pair up. Just give me the cards." He gave her the cards. Rhoda went to the police station and persuaded one of the young police officers to help her find the houses. The young officer would knock on the door, and when the startled prospects answered it, the policeman would present Rhoda Burdeshaw, and she would invite them to church. Every person she visited came to church the next Sunday.

Years later, Dr. Hinson went back to that same church to preach a revival. On the first night, the sanctuary was packed. The church was vibrant and alive and making an impact on the community. Dr. Hinson told them that the first person he saw was someone who was not even there, someone who is now in heaven, but he could still see her sitting on the third pew with a Bible in one hand and her visitation flashlight in the other, ready to illuminate that community with the light of Christ.

If we are going to build the church on the foundation of Jesus Christ, then we must be what Jesus called us to be, salt that brings flavor to the world and light that illuminates the world's darkness. In order to do that, we must infiltrate the community.

Then we must *present Jesus* to the people we meet as we infiltrate the community. Our light will not illuminate their darkness; the light of Christ will. Our love will not transform people's lives; the love of Christ will. We do not go out in our name; we go out in the name of Jesus Christ. We have nothing to offer the world that will make an eternal difference in their lives except him. Jesus is our message. If, after we have prayed for the harvest and infiltrated the community, we do nothing more than make church members out of them, then we have failed in our mission. The church's mission is to bring people into a relationship with Jesus Christ so their spiritual needs can be met in and through him and so they can become engaged in kingdom work.

10

All Things Are Yours

1 Corinthians 3:18-23

The Christians in Corinth face a daunting task. Paul leaves them in Corinth to plant the church of Jesus Christ in a hostile environment. They do not have the stability produced by a long and rich history. They do not have the strength supplied by a favored position in society. They do not have the status provided by influential leaders in the community. Nevertheless, without that stability or strength or status, Paul challenges the Christians in Corinth to plant the church of Jesus Christ. They face a daunting task. Up to this point, they are not very effective in carrying out their assignment. Often they seem to be more influenced by the world than vice versa. Instead of being light to illuminate the darkness, they let the shadows of darkness fall across their behavior. Instead of demonstrating a new community in Christ, they reflect the same conflicting relationships that characterize the pagan Corinthian culture.

These Corinthian Christians are called by God and assigned by Paul to plant the church of Jesus Christ in the pagan, immoral, materialistic city of Corinth, and they are not very effective in carrying out their assignment. They are apparently stymied by two misconceptions.

On the one hand, the Christians at Corinth *overestimate what they bring to the table* (vv. 18-21a). In other words, they think too highly of themselves. They are like the foreman of a new project who explains to his workers what he wants them to accomplish and when he wants them to accomplish it. When he finishes his speech, one of the workers protests, "We do not need to push so hard, do we? After all, Rome wasn't built in a day." To which the man responds, "That is because I was not the foreman."

Sometimes we make that mistake in the church. We think that if we can develop the right organization, follow the right strategy, or perfect the right methodology, then we can build the church for God. We fall prey to what we can call "an idolatry of technique." That problem plagues the church at Corinth. The Corinthian Christians simply duplicate the patterns of the world, thinking that the wisdom of the world will equip them to build the church for Jesus Christ.

Paul counters that overconfidence with a warning: *Do not deceive yourselves. If any one of you thinks he is wise by the standards of this age, he should become a 'fool' so that he may become wise. For the wisdom of this world is foolishness in God's sight* (vv. 18-19). Paul supports his conclusion with two quotes from the Old Testament, one from Job 5:12-13 and the other from Psalm 94:11. The first reveals that human beings in their craftiness are no match for God, and the second reveals that nothing that enters the human mind matches up to God's understanding. Paul warns the Corinthian Christians against relying too much on their own abilities.

The other problem is more serious. The Christians at Corinth *underestimate what God brings to the table* (vv. 21b-23). In other words, they overlook the vast spiritual resources God makes available to them. They are like a farmer and his wife who live in abject poverty for years without knowing that a bountiful pocket of oil exists beneath their barren, dusty land. After they discover the oil and begin to reap their resources, the farmer says to his wife, "To think, we lived here all these years without knowing how rich we were!"

Sometimes we make that mistake in the church. God cannot do anything spectacular in our church, we think. God cannot change lives in our church. God cannot do any miracles in our church. We fall prey to what we might call "practicing atheism." That is, we claim to believe in God, but we really do not. Henry Blackaby, who developed the concept of "Experiencing God," put it this way: "When you believe that nothing significant can happen through you, you have said more about your belief in God than you have said about yourself."[1]

That problem also plagues the church at Corinth. They lose their vision of God, forgetting that he is the one who holds the whole world in his hands and the one who is able to do immeasurably more than we even ask or think. So Paul writes in verses 22-23, *All things are yours, whether Paul or Apollos or Cephas or the world or life or death or the present or the future—all are yours, and you are of Christ, and Christ is of God.* Paul reminds the Corinthian Christians about the unlimited resources God makes available to them.

Overestimating what we bring to the table and underestimating what God brings to the table are two problems that stymie the church at Corinth and still plague the church today. I will illustrate what often happens in the church. A car skids on a wet spot on the interstate and then rolls over and comes to a stop back on its wheels. The driver, obviously shaken up, opens the door, gets out of the car, walks over to the grassy area beside the shoulder of the road, and collapses. The woman in the following car stops to assist the injured man. Soon a man rushes up to the scene, pushing the woman away. "Move over, lady," he shouts, "I've had a first aid course." The woman steps back and watches for a few minutes. Finally, she tells the man, "When you get to the part in your training where it says, 'Call a doctor,' I'll be right over here."

We often do that to God in the church. We push God to the side and tell him, "Move over. I have had a leadership course." We become so busy applying our techniques that we fail to hear the divine whisper: "When you get to the part where it says, 'Call on God,' I'll be right over here." An idolatry of technique—overestimating what we bring to the table—is a common problem in the church.

But I think the more serious problem that plagues the church today is our tendency to underestimate what God brings to the table. We often trivialize God. We forget who God really is and what God can do.

I heard Fred Craddock tell in a sermon about a time when he visited a woman who was seriously ill. Her husband called Fred to the house to pray for her. Fred stood at the end of the bed and prayed that God might take away her illness and heal her. As soon as he finished his prayer, the woman opened her eyes, pushed the covers back, stood up, put on her robe, and invited Fred and her husband to the kitchen, where she made some coffee for them. Fred said he was so shook up he ran outside and looked up to the heavens and screamed, "God, don't you ever to that to me again!" Do we really want God to do something spectacular, or would we be scared to death if something happened that we could not explain in terms of our own ability?

A few days after Blaise Pascal's death in 1662, a servant happened to find hidden in the lining of his master's coat a piece of parchment paper covered with the philosopher's writing. For eight years Pascal had kept close to his heart this testimony to a life-changing encounter:

In the year of Grace, 1654,
On Monday, 23rd of November, Feast of St. Clement,
Pope and Martyr, and of others in the Martyrology,
Vigil of Saint Chrysogonus, martyr and others,
From about half past ten in the evening
until about half past twelve

FIRE
God of Abraham, God of Isaac, God of Jacob
not of the philosophers and scholars
Certitude. Certitude. Feeling. Joy. Peace.
God of Jesus Christ.[2]

Have we had that kind of life-changing experience with God that set our lives on fire, or is ours merely a religion of routine and ritual? Do we really believe in God? I am talking about the creator God, the sovereign God, the all-powerful God, and the transforming God—the God who delivered Israel from Egypt, the God who raised Jesus from the grave, and the God who empowered the first-century church. Do we really believe in God, or is it all just talk?

As the Hebrew refugees from Egypt stand on the threshold of the land of Canaan that God promised to their father Abraham, they have behind them a history of extraordinary interventions by God, including the ten plagues from the hand of this sovereign God that finally broke down the resolve of Pharaoh and led to their release from Egypt and God's guidance through the wilderness. They have sworn their allegiance to God, and now, as they stand at the threshold of their promised land, they send their spies to bring back a plan for taking possession of Canaan. However, the report from the spies is not what they expect. The spies tell of giants in the land and fortified cities and powerful obstacles. "We can't attack those people," they report to the people, "for they are stronger than we are." Two of the spies—Joshua and Caleb—urge the people to enter the promised land with the assurance that the God to whom they pledged allegiance, the God who promised them power, will go before them to bring them to victory. But the Hebrews listen to their fears instead of their faith and refuse to take possession of the land. As a result, they miss their opportunity. Why? Because they claim to believe in God but really do not believe in him (Num 13).

Centuries later the disciples, the twelve minus Judas, join with other believers, men and women—120 of them in all. As they stand on the threshold of their promised land, they too have behind them a history of extraordinary interventions by God, chief among them the resurrection of Jesus from death. They have sworn their allegiance to God, and now, on the threshold of their promised land, they evaluate the challenges facing them. They have no reputation. They have no standing in society. They have no financial resources. They have no personal power. The inescapable conclusion from this quick review should have been, "We can't take possession of the world for Christ. There is no way. The only thing we will get from going out into the community with the gospel is our own death." But these disciples listen to their faith instead of their fear, and they turn the world upside down. As a result, they seize their opportunity. Why? Because they claim to believe in God and really do believe in him (see Acts 1).

In the year of our Lord, 2011, people of faith again stand on the threshold of a promised land, a world hungry for the gospel of Jesus Christ. We have behind us a history of extraordinary interventions by God. How will we respond to our opportunity? Will we listen to our fear (like the Hebrews), or will we listen to our faith (like the first disciples)? Or, to express it a different way, do we really believe in God, or is it all just talk?

Notes

1. Henry T. Blackaby and Claude V. King, *Experiencing God* (Nashville: Broadman & Holman Publishers, 1994) 29.

2. Donald W. McCullough, *The Trivialization of God* (Colorado Springs: Navpress, 1995) 77.

11

Found Faithful

1 Corinthians 4:1-5

He was on the pastor search committee that called me to one of my churches. He had previously served as president of the state Baptist convention, one of the only laymen ever to be selected to such a position in the state. He had also served in various positions of leadership in our church. However, the defining moment of his life was his success as a businessman. Just before I went to the church as pastor, he sold his business for several million dollars. Partly because of how he used his new wealth—he now had a house in North Carolina to check on and a house on the coast to check on—and partly because he was now retired, this church member was suddenly gone most weekends. I tried to keep him connected to the church, but he was never there. He dropped out of all his leadership roles. Eventually he quit coming to church at all. That is a common problem in the church in every century.

In the first century church it was Demas. At one time Demas was Paul's "beloved" fellow worker (Col 4:14). However, later in his letter to young Timothy, Paul says this about Demas: "Demas, because he loved this world, has deserted me" (2 Tim 4:10).

In our day, thousands just like the church member mentioned above, men and women who are at one time on fire for the Lord, rise up as leaders of the people of God but then fall away and end up as alumni of the church.

Why does this happen? Sometimes people fall away because of *spiritual depletion*. Like having bank accounts from which we continually withdraw money but into which we never make deposits, many Christians never make deposits into their spiritual bank accounts but constantly expend spiritual energy until one day they discover they are out of spiritual capital.

Sometimes people fall away because of *physical exhaustion*. Serving others in Jesus' name requires energy and is often exhausting. Have you heard this twist on a popular poem from our childhood?

Mary had a little lamb
'Twas given her to keep
But then she joined the Baptist church
And died from lack of sleep.

Sometimes people fall away because of *hurt feelings*. Criticism is inevitable in the Christian life. The key is how we respond to it. One pastor gave good advice when he said, "Never be afraid of honest criticism. If the critic is wrong, you can help him; and if you're wrong, he can help you. Either way, somebody's helped." Unfortunately, we do not always take that high road in response to criticism. Sometimes we allow the criticism to sour our attitude toward the Lord and drive us away from the church.

Sometimes people fall away because of *a smug satisfaction with what they have already accomplished*. What often sidetracks Christians is not the despair that comes from failing to reach our goals but the hubris that comes when we do reach our goals. Larry Christenson puts it like this: "The greatest indictment of a Christian congregation is not that it is falling short of the mark but that it has quit striving to reach the mark."[1]

For one reason or another, many have slipped away from the church. When pastors fall away, this apostasy is usually widely publicized, but when it happens to laypeople, little publicity is given to it. No public resignation is read. The former leader just fades into the woodwork. One day, in a conversation of people at church, someone raises the question: "Whatever happened to . . . Demas?"

Again, this problem has plagued the church in every century. Strong church members have fallen away and become alumni. Paul faces the same problem in the Corinthian church, so he writes this [part of the] letter to remind the Corinthian Christians of some important truths.

To begin with, Paul wants the Corinthian Christians *to remember who they are*. He writes in verse 1, *So then men ought to regard us as servants of Christ*. The Greek word translated "servant" literally means an under-rower on a war ship, one who rows under the orders of a supervisor. Eventually the word described any person who received orders from a higher authority. That is who we are, Paul declares, "servants of Christ"—men and women who operate under the orders of a higher authority.

Servants do not decide when they will work. Instead, they work according to the orders of their supervisor. Servants do not decide what they will do. Instead, they do what their supervisor instructs them to do. Servants do not decide how they will do their work. Instead, they follow the example and the instructions of their supervisor. Servants are simply responsible to obey their supervisor, and the Bible says that is who we are, "servants of Christ."

Paul also wants the Corinthian Christians *to remember the responsibility God has given to them*. He reminds the Corinthian Christians that they have been *entrusted with the secret things of God* (v. 1). In the King James Version, this verse identifies us as *stewards of the mysteries of God*. A steward is the chief household servant to whom the master entrusts all his resources. Yet the steward does not just enjoy those resources himself. Instead, he responsibly distributes the resources of the master to all the other servants.

That is who we are: distributors of the resources of God. All of God's provisions have been put at our disposal, but we are not just to enjoy these resources ourselves. Instead, we are to distribute the resources of the master responsibly to all the other servants.

In addition, Paul wants the Christians at Corinth *to remember what is expected of them*. He affirms, *Now it is required that those who have been given a trust must prove faithful* (v. 2). We are not required to be successful. We are not required to be the best. We are simply required to be faithful. Faithfulness means to keep obeying Jesus, to keep sharing his resources with others, and to keep living for him. We might also express the central truth of Paul's word in this way: to be faithful means simply to do the best we can for as long as we can.

Most of all, Paul wants the Christians at Corinth *to remember their accountability to God*. He issues this warning to the Corinthians: *He will bring to light what is hidden in darkness and will expose the motives of men's hearts. At that time each will receive his praise from God* (v. 5). We can never accurately judge another person because we are limited in our perspective. That is why Paul asserts, *I care very little if I am judged by you or by any human court* (v. 3). And we can never accurately judge ourselves because our conscience can easily be deceived. That is why Paul adds, *I do not even judge myself* (v. 3). Yet we cannot escape the judgment of God, for God sees all and knows all. Someday we will have to explain to God what we have done with the resources he has entrusted to us. Servants of God who are responsible to distribute God's riches to the world, who are expected to be faithful, and who will someday have to give an account of their lives to God—that is who the Corinthian Christians are.

And that is who we are as Christians today. We are servants of God, nothing more and nothing less. We have been given the unique responsibility of distributing the riches of God's grace to all who are around us, and God requires only one thing of us—that we be faithful, that we keep obeying him week end and week out year after year, and that we keep distributing the riches of his grace to those around us. Someday we will have to stand before God and give an account of how we have carried out our responsibility as members of the family of God.

How should we respond to the truths presented in our text? Let me offer two words.

The first word is *enthusiasm*. Because of who we are and because of what God has called us to do, we must be enthusiastic about the work of the church. Let me illustrate what this looks like.

Several years ago, Marriott Hotels gave their annual award for best sports salesperson to Albert "Smitty" Smith, the room service captain at the Atlanta Marriott. When he accepted his award, he told the audience, "I'm not really a salesperson. My job is to take care of the sports teams when they come to town. I work twenty-four hours a day to meet their every wish. Even when the Dodgers switched to another hotel for a cheaper rate, I still wanted to help them out. One time when the Dodgers came to town I met them in their new hotel. I told manager Tommy Lasorda that even though they were staying at a new hotel, I was going to bring over their special order from the Marriott after the game. Lasorda asked why I would do such a thing and I explained that the room service at this new hotel closes at eleven p.m. and if the game goes into extra innings, they will miss their late-night snack. I also explained to him that even though the Dodgers could not afford to stay at the Marriott anymore, we still loved them."[2] Paul calls us to display that same kind of enthusiasm about the work of God.

The other word is *persistence*. Because of who we are and because of what God has called us to do, we must make a covenant of obedience with God that causes us to say, "Whatever God has called me to do, I will continue to do it with passion for as long as I am able." Again, let me illustrate what this looks like.

The NCAA championship game in 1983 when North Carolina State upset the highly favored Houston team stands as one of the unforgettable sports moments in college basketball. No one who witnessed it can forget the picture of North Carolina Coach Jimmy Valvano running out on the court with both hands in the air looking for someone to hug. A few years after that championship season, cancer struck Coach Jimmy V, and he died in 1993 at the age of forty-seven. A few weeks before he died, a group of his friends honored Valvano. The recognition service played on national television, and to that vast viewing audience, Jimmy V said, "Cancer has taken away a lot of my physical abilities. Cancer is attacking and destroying my body. But what cancer cannot touch is my mind, my heart, and my soul. I have faith in God . . . and hope that things might get better for me. But even if they don't I promise you this. I will never ever give up. I will never ever quit. . . ." Then, pointing to his 1983 championship team, he said, "I learned a great lesson from these guys; they amazed me! They did things I wasn't sure they could do because they absolutely refused to give up! That was the theme of our championship season, 'Never give up!' That's the lesson I learned from them and that's the message I leave with you: 'Never give up. Never ever give up.'"[3] Paul calls us to display that kind of persistence about the work of God.

We are servants of God who are responsible to distribute God's riches to the world, who are expected to be faithful, and who will someday have to give an account of our lives to God.

Notes

1. Larry Christenson, *Back to Square One* (Minneapolis: Bethany Fellowship, 1979) 54.

2. Roger Dow and Susan Cook, *Turned On* (New York: HarperBusiness, 1996) 234–35.

3. James W. Moore. *Attitude Is Your Paintbrush* (Nashville: Dimensions for Living, 1998) 64.

12

Fools for Christ

1 Corinthians 4:6-13

Popular writer Philip Yancey has come into contact with many Christian musicians, artists, and authors over the years. The lives of these Christian individuals are characterized by great creativity. But, Yancey says, these creative people are not all the same. Yancey lumps them into two sets: Christian entertainers and Christian servants. Christian entertainers are musicians, actors, writers, speakers, and comedians who fill our periodicals and dominate our seminars and appear on our television screens. They have fame, prestige, and money, but many, Yancey suggests, also have deep longings and self-doubts. Christian servants, on the other hand, are rarely in the spotlight. They toil unnoticed in remote places. They live among the rejects of society and work for low pay, long hours, and no applause. Their talents and skills are given to the poor and uneducated. Yet, somehow, in the process of losing their lives, they have found them and attained rewards that the famous never experience.[1]

Yancey's distinction between Christian entertainers and Christian servants introduces a problem in today's church. According to the Apostle Paul, this distinction between Christian entertainers and Christian servants also appears in the first-century church.

Some in the Corinthian church apparently see themselves as what Yancey calls Christian entertainers. Paul addresses them in verse 8: *Already you have all you want! Already you have become rich! You have become kings— and that without us!* Paul's contemporaries in Corinth use the word "king" to designate wealthy patrons, those on the higher end of the social scale. So when Paul says some of the Christians in Corinth "have become kings," he means they have position and prestige and power. They are Christian entertainers.

Paul contrasts these Christian entertainers with the other group, ones whom Yancey identifies as Christian servants. Listen to the description of these Christian servants beginning in verse 11:

> To this very hour we go hungry and thirsty, we are in rags, we are brutally treated, we are homeless. We work hard with our own hands. When we are cursed, we bless; when we are persecuted, we endure it; when we are slandered, we answer kindly. Up to this moment we have become the scum of the earth, the refuse of the world.

Unlike the entertainers, these Christian servants have no position and no prestige and no power. Instead, they can be characterized by terms like fools, scum of the earth, refuse of the world. Yancey's distinction between Christian entertainers and Christian servants provides a precise backdrop for Paul's discussion in our text.

Let me ask you a question. Which would you rather be: kings or the scum of the earth?

That is the problem, isn't it? The desire for prestige, position, and power resides in each of us. We do not really want to be the scum of the earth. We prefer to be kings. These inner desires often prevent us from filling our proper role as servants of Christ.

Some of you know the story of Alf Wright. He quietly carried out his career as a veterinarian in Yorkshire, England, until at the age of fifty-three, when all of that changed with the publication of his book, *All Creatures Great and Small*. This book was so successful that it catapulted him to worldwide fame under the pen name James Herriot. Several years later, a friend listened to him present a speech to the Booksellers Association Conference and was amazed at how he had developed as a speaker. Herriot perfectly timed his speech, bringing together his humorous stories that caused the crowd to roar with approval. At the end, they leaped to their feet and gave him a standing ovation. After the speech, his friend said, "Alf, that was marvelous. Remember what it was like in Newcastle all those years ago? You've timed it perfectly. It's absolutely lovely now." Alf, better known as James Herriot, responded to his friend, "Aye, Dick, it's a heady brew, and I'm giving it up." And he never gave another speech.[2]

Our position as Christians can create the same tension within us. To have a personal relationship with God, to be called to a special assignment by God himself, to have the mysteries of God revealed to us, and to be entrusted with the gospel—all of that can be a "heady brew," as James Herriot puts it.

Instead of being servants of Christ, we can morph into Christian entertainers, and instead of magnifying God's glory in our lives, we can end up seeking to magnify our own.

What can we do to resist that temptation? Paul gives a couple of suggestions in our text. He provides the first suggestion in verse 6: *Now, brothers, I have applied these things to myself and Apollos for your benefit, so that you may learn from us the meaning of the saying, 'Do not go beyond what is written.' Then you will not take pride in one man over against another.*

Exactly what does this verse mean? Scholars debate about "these things" that Paul applies to himself and Apollos. What are "these things"? Scholars also wonder what Paul alludes to when he says, "Do not go beyond what is written." Instead of getting into an extended discussion of these terms, let me summarize what I think this verse says. By "these things," Paul refers to the Old Testament Scriptures he has quoted in the preceding verses (1:19; 1:31; 2:9; 3:19; 3:20), and with the saying, "Do not go beyond what is written," Paul tells the Corinthian Christians not to move beyond what is written in those Scriptures that he has quoted.

What do these Scriptures say? If you study these allusions Paul makes to Isaiah, Jeremiah, Job, and Psalms, you will discover that the cumulative impact of those verses places a strict limit on human pride and calls for trust in God alone. Remember that, Paul tells the Corinthians. Live by that.

Let me provide an illustration of someone who demonstrates what Paul describes in our text. German Christian Dietrich Bonhoeffer's career bloomed most brightly in the 1930s. He was brilliant and gifted and charismatic. We can call him a Christian entertainer, but then something happened that transformed him into a humble servant of the Lord who eventually gave his life for the cause of Christ. What prompted that transformation? This is his explanation, written in a letter to a friend in 1936: "I threw myself into work in a very unchristian way. An . . . ambition that many people noticed in me, made my life difficult. . . . Then something happened, something that has changed and transformed my life right up to the present day. I discovered the Bible for the first time."[3] Bonhoeffer changed from a Christian entertainer into a Christian servant by remembering the word of God, just as Paul suggests in our text. Bonhoeffer made the decision not to "go beyond what is written." Remember what is written in God's word. That is Paul's first suggestion in verse 6.

He offers a second suggestion in verse 7 with a series of three questions: *For who makes you different from anyone else? What do you have that you did not receive? And if you did receive it, why do you boast as though you did not?* The first question is simply this: "Who has distinguished you from those who are around you?" The implied answer is: "God has." God is the one who saves them (1:19). God is the one who chooses them (1:27-28). God is the one who reveals to them the hidden mysteries (2:10-12). God is the one who gifts them (12:6). God is the one who gives them the final victory over death (15:57). Everything that makes them special has been provided by God. "Who has distinguished you from those who are around you?" Paul asks the Corinthians. He gives this answer: "God has." The second question provides a slight variation on the first question: "What do you have that you did not receive?" The implied answer is, "Nothing." The answers to these two questions lead to the third question: "If everything special about you is provided by God, and if you have nothing that you did not receive from God, then what are you bragging about?" The only one you need to brag about is God. Remember that, Paul tells the Corinthians. Live by that.

Here is a picture of what that means: When Rodney Smith was a little boy traveling across England in a wagon with a gypsy band, he made spending money by whittling clothespins from sticks and selling them at houses along the road and in the villages. As a teenager, he heard the gospel and was saved. His whole life changed. He became a preacher and eventually a world-famous evangelist known as Gypsy Smith. He traveled around the world several times. He conducted evangelistic campaigns in large cities. The notables of his day entertained him. Thousands came to Christ through his preaching. When people visited his home in England, they saw an old pruning knife that Gypsy Smith kept in a place of honor in the living room. He told his visitors that he left that knife there for a reason. Sometimes, as he grew older, he said he was inclined to feel a little proud and puffed up because of his success. Whenever that happened, he would pick up that old knife and say to himself, "Old man, this is what you came from. This is where the Lord found you—with that knife in your hand making clothespins for a miserable living. There is nothing in you to be proud of: you owe everything to God's tender grace and loving mercy."[4] Gypsy Smith was kept from becoming a Christian entertainer by the reminder that everything special about him came through the provision of God. Remember where you came from. That is Paul's second suggestion in verse 7.

What could the Corinthian Christians do to keep from becoming Christian entertainers instead of Christian servants? Remember the word, and live by it. Remember where you came from, and thank God for it. That is Paul's advice to the Corinthian Christians in our text. This good advice echoes across the centuries to us today.

Notes

1. Philip Yancey, *Open Windows* (Westchester IL: Crossway Books, 1982) 212–13.

2. Graham Lord, *James Herriot: The Life of a Country Vet* (New York: Carroll & Graf Publishers, 1997) 188.

3. Eberhard Bethge, *Bonhoeffer*, trans. Rosaleen Ockenden (London: Fount Paperbacks, 1979) 35.

4. *Proclaim: The Pastor's Journal for Biblical Preaching* 5/3 (April–June 1975): 32.

13

Motivations for Ministry

1 Corinthians 4:14-21

Robert B. Cialdini, a professor at Arizona State University, has done a provocative study on how we influence people to do things. He cites six rules that are most effective in motivating others. The *Rule of Reciprocation* creates a sense of obligation. Someone gives us a book or a flower or a gift, and then we feel obligated to give something in return. The *Rule of Commitment* binds people to past decisions regardless of whether those decisions are still relevant or wise. Get a person to make a commitment and then repeatedly remind them that they must be faithful to their promise. The *Rule of Social Proof* grows out of the tendency of people to do what they see others doing. Most people would rather imitate than initiate, so you get someone to lead the way and others will follow. The *Rule of Liking* is the practice of using friendly, warm, or famous people to pitch a product. Our warm feeling toward the person transfers to a warm feeling toward the product. The *Rule of Authority* is the influence caused by people in power or who have position. If these authority figures act in a certain way, many will follow in their path. The *Rule of Scarcity* motivates us by suggesting the scarcity of something. Whenever our freedom to have something is limited, our desire for it greatly increases.[1]

Each of us can probably think of particular instances when these various techniques came into play, either used on us or applied by us. Sometimes these actions morph from motivations into manipulations, to be sure. Nevertheless, according to Cialdini, these are ways in which we motivate people to do things.

Motivation is of course important in every area of life. I have heard several people attribute an often-told story to Bear Bryant when he coached at Texas A&M University. His quarterback for the year ran slower than anyone on the team, but he made up for his lack of speed with a quick arm and extraordinary passing accuracy. The quarterback never ran the ball. He just threw it or handed it off to someone else. In one game, Texas A&M led by only six points with less than two minutes left in the game. They had the ball, and Coach Bryant wanted to run out the clock. He called a time out and brought the quarterback to the sideline. He told him he wanted him to do a simple handoff and run out the clock. The quarterback went back to the huddle and altered the coach's instructions. He told his team, "Coach wants us to play it safe, run out the clock, but that's what the other team is expecting us to do. Let's surprise them with a quick pass over the middle." The huddle broke. The play unfolded. The quarterback passed the ball, and a streaking defensive back—the fastest man on the other team—intercepted the pass and headed for the other end zone for what would be the winning touchdown. The quarterback started after him and amazingly caught up with him and tackled him just before he crossed the goal line. The game clock ran out, and the A & M football team preserved their victory. After the game, the press asked Coach Bryant to explain how the slowest man on his team ran down the fastest man on the other team and tackled him before he scored. Bryant responded, "It's really quite simple. It's a matter of motivation. The one who intercepted the pass was running for a touchdown, but my quarterback, who threw a pass in disobedience to my orders, was running for his life!" Motivation is important.

Paul understands the importance of motivation, and he uses a variety of techniques in his personal ministry and in his letters to influence other people to live out their lives for Christ. In our text for this chapter, Paul uses two specific techniques to influence the Christians at Corinth.

The first technique, in verses 14-17, is *modeling*. Paul tells the Corinthians, *I spent a year and a half in Corinth* [Acts 18:11], *living out the Christian life. Follow my example.* In other words, do what you saw me doing. Paul knows people will do what they see modeled effectively before their own eyes.

Let us unpack that idea. The "guardians" identified in verse 15 are special servants who guard the children until they are ready to go to the teachers. The guardians try to keep the children safe, and sometimes they use severe methods to accomplish their task. Drawings on some ancient Greek vases uncovered by archaeologists picture these guardians with sticks in their hands. Some people translate the word "guardian" as "disciplinarian." By the use of shame and heavy discipline, these guardians attempt to keep their charges in line.

Against that background, Paul suggests to the Corinthians, *You can find someone like that on every corner. There are 10,000 of them.* Perhaps we can translate that word "gazillion"! There are a gazillion of them. *But,* Paul adds, *that is not the approach I take. I am not a guardian brandishing the rod with heavy discipline trying to bring you in line. Instead,* Paul concludes, *I am your father who sets an example for you to follow.* That metaphor precisely describes the relationship between Paul and the Corinthian Christians. He is their father in the faith, for he birthed the church, he led the individual members of the Corinthian congregation to the Lord, and then he trained them for eighteen months. He is their spiritual father.

Based on that unique relationship, Paul then challenges the Corinthian Christians, *Therefore I urge you to imitate me* (v. 16). That statement bothers us to a degree, particularly coming right after his discussion of those who want to be kings elevating themselves above everyone else (4:6-13). *Imitate me,* Paul says. He does not say "imitate Christ" but instead says *Imitate me.* What are we to make of that statement? In Paul's defense, we first need to acknowledge *what* he asks them to imitate. Paul asks them to imitate him as a servant of Christ, not as a Christian entertainer. Paul asks them to imitate him as a fool for Christ, not as one considered to be wise by the world. Paul asks them to imitate him as the scum of the earth, not as a king. Because of what he asks them to imitate, to be "Paul-like" simply means to be "Christ-like." That removes some of the egotistical edge from Paul's request.

Paul also understands the importance of having a flesh-and-blood demonstration of what the Christian life looks like. Denis Waitley changes Edgar A. Guest's famous poem "Sermons We See" to say, "I'd rather watch a winner, than hear one any day." Albert Einstein expresses this truth even more succinctly when he declares, "Setting an example is not the main means of influencing another, it is the *only* means."[2]

Paul understands that principle. So instead of simply telling the Corinthian Christians how they should live, he shows them. Then he says, "Imitate me." Paul attempts to motivate the Corinthian Christians by the principle of modeling.

The second technique, in verses 18-21, is the principle of *accountability.* Paul says in effect, "I've put you in charge of contextualizing the gospel in the pagan, immoral city of Corinth. Someday I am going to return to Corinth and we are going to have a show and tell." Paul knows people will do what they are held accountable for.

I heard about a person in Massachusetts a number of years ago who perfectly understood the principle of accountability. Christian Herter served as the governor of the state of Massachusetts at the time. He appeared at the annual state legislative barbecue after a day of heavy campaigning. He did not have time to eat, so when he arrived at the barbecue around six o'clock he was famished. He stood in the food line with everybody else, and when he reached the front he said to the serving lady, "Do you mind if I take a second piece of chicken?" "I'm sorry," she said. "It's one to a customer." "But I'm starving," Herter explained. "Sorry, mister," the lady said. "One to a customer. That's the rule." "Do you know who I am?" he said. "I am the governor of this state." Without blinking an eye, she returned, "And do you know who I am? I'm the lady in charge of the chicken."[3]

That lady understood the principle of accountability. Being accountable for what happened to the chicken motivated her to do the job right. Paul applies that principle to the Christians in Corinth. They have been left in Corinth not just to talk the talk but also to walk the walk. Apparently, some of them do a good job at talking their faith but not at living their faith. Apparently they neglect their responsibility to live the faith because they believe Paul will never come back to Corinth and thus they will never have to give an answer for the way they live. Paul warns them that he will return, and as their spiritual father he will either come with a whip to bring them into shape or with the spirit of a father who is proud of his children. In issuing this warning, Paul attempts to motivate the Corinthian Christians by the principle of accountability.

Paul uses both the principle of modeling and the principle of accountability to motivate the Christians at Corinth. However, we need to remember that Paul has more concern about the product of these strategies than about the strategies themselves. What does Paul model before the people? What does he want them to do? He wants them to become servants of Christ who are faithful to God. He motivates them to do ministry.

Why is this important? Remember again what the Bible says about ministry. The Bible affirms that we are created for ministry (Eph 2:10), saved for ministry (2 Tim 1:9), called to ministry (1 Pet 2:9-10), gifted for ministry (1 Pet 4:10), commanded to do ministry (Matt 20:26-28), needed for ministry (1 Cor 12:27), and accountable for ministry (Col 3:23-24).

Paul's challenge comes across the years to twenty-first-century Christians as well. Our greatest challenge as Christians today is to find out what God wants us to do and to do it, because this is who we are: servants of Christ, stewards of the mysteries of God, and called to be faithful like the Apostle Paul. Paul expresses this central truth about the Christian life at the beginning of chapter 4: "So then, men ought to regard us as servants of Christ and as those entrusted with the secret things of God. Now it is required that those who have been given a trust must prove faithful" (1 Cor 4:1).

Notes

1. David L. Larsen, *The Anatomy of Preaching* (Grand Rapids MI: Kregel Publications, 1989) 139–41.

2. Denis Waitley, *Ten Seeds of Greatness* (Old Tappan NJ: Fleming H. Revell Co., 1983) 209; Ted W. Engstrom, *Motivation to Last a Lifetime* (Grand Rapids MI: Zondervan Publishing House, 1984) 69.

3. William Novak, *Man of the House: The Life and Political Memoirs of Speaker Tip O'Neill* (New York: Random House, 1987) 42.

14

Weeds in God's Garden

1 Corinthians 5:1–13

Jeb Stuart McGruder was one of the key figures in the Watergate scandal. A rising young politician with a good background and a promising future, McGruder became confused about the distinction between right and wrong and was caught up in the Watergate coverup. When the court sentenced him to prison, someone asked him why he became involved in that crime. He appraised, "My ambition obscured my judgment. Somewhere between my ambition and my ideals I lost my compass."[1]

Something similar takes place in the church at Corinth. As a result, a blatant example of immorality emerges inside the church that exceeds the immorality outside the church. Remember the cultural context of the Corinthian church. This ancient city of nearly 500,000 people has a reputation for its immorality. A common proverb of that day suggests that not every person should go to Corinth, meaning that not every person can withstand the temptation oozing out of this immoral city. In that corrupt place, Paul calls Christians to live a controlled, disciplined, holy lifestyle. He wants them to be Christ-like. Instead, some of them are actually more "Corinthian-like." They lose their moral compass. Paul addresses that problem in this chapter.

It is actually reported, Paul begins, *that there is sexual immorality among you* (v. 1). Then Paul cites a particular case of immorality. Even though he does not mention the person's name, the Corinthians can immediately identify the culprit. This flagrant immorality provides the main topic of discussion in the sidewalk committee meetings of First Church in Corinth. As a Christian, this man to whom Paul refers has been called to a life of holiness and purity. Instead, he lives in blatant immorality, and everyone in the church knows it.

This is no ordinary example of immorality but one that stuns Paul when he hears about it. This immorality spoiling the fellowship of the church in

Corinth, Paul asserts, *is of a kind that does not occur even among the pagans* (v. 1). A member of the Corinthian church gets involved in a sexual tryst with his father's wife. The word for this shocking immorality is "incest." Jewish law specifically forbids incest (Lev 18:6). Even Roman law forbids such behavior. Yet, the church in Corinth winks at what the Jewish law forbids and the pagan world prohibits. Even when they become aware of this blatant example of immorality, the Corinthian church folks refuse to deal with it. When Paul hears about it, he explodes in disbelief. Then he recommends a plan for excising this spiritual cancer from the church at Corinth.

What is Paul's plan? He urges the Corinthians, *Hand this man over to Satan, so that the sinful nature may be destroyed and his spirit saved on the day of the Lord* (v. 5). What does that mean? The plan proposed by Paul includes both a means and an end.

The *means* for dealing with the problem is to deliver the man to Satan. This is probably a strong term for excommunication from the church. Paul therefore instructs the Corinthian church to put this man who is guilty of such shocking immorality out of the church and into the world where Satan rules.

What is the *end* result Paul hopes to accomplish with this strategy? Paul wants the sinner's "nature" to be destroyed and his "spirit" to be saved. "Nature" is the old sinful nature from which we have been redeemed. "Spirit" is the new spiritual nature given to us as Christians. So Paul hopes through the means of excommunication to bring about a redemptive result in this man. He wants to put him out of the church so that, when this man becomes aware of the error of his ways and when he realizes how much he is missing that Christ could give him, he will come to his senses. He will then repent and turn back to the fellowship of the church.

All of this seems clear-cut on the surface. However, another passage in another New Testament book suggests a different strategy for dealing with a transgression by a church member. In the sixth chapter of Galatians, Paul refers to a person who not only sins but is "caught in a sin." The implication of that phrase is that the person's sin has become public knowledge. How are other Christians to respond? To the Corinthians, Paul declares, "Put him out of the church." But in his Galatian epistle, Paul recommends another approach. He calls on the church to restore the person who has fallen into sin. In Galatians 6:1, Paul instructs the churches in Galatia, "Brothers, if someone is caught in a sin, you who are spiritual should restore him gently." The verb translated "restore" is a medical term used for setting a fractured bone. Something is out of joint in the life of this Christian. The proper response is to set it straight.

To the Corinthians, Paul says concerning a person caught in sin: throw him out. To the Galatians, Paul advises concerning a person caught in sin: restore him. How can we reconcile these two apparently contradictory commands?

Perhaps we can understand these contrasting commands as being shaped by the different contexts in which Paul issues them. The church in Corinth is in one of the most immoral cities of the ancient world. Perhaps to counter the immorality rampant in Corinth, Paul urges instantaneous action toward this person involved in an incestuous relationship. In the province of Galatia, perhaps these issues of rampant immorality do not predominate in the same way as they do in Corinth. Consequently, Paul does not demand the same rigorous reaction. Perhaps different settings evoke the different advice.

Or perhaps we can understand these contrasting commands as being given at different stages of the church's relationship with this person involved in sin. Paul's advice to the Galatians, perhaps, comes early in the process where Paul hopes an attitude of compassion will invoke repentance in the guilty party so he can be quickly restored. But in the Corinthian situation, perhaps the church member involved in the sinful behavior rebuffs the early attempt at compassion. The man continues in his sin. Finally, Paul realizes the church has no other option but to kick him out. Perhaps difference in timing brings forth from Paul the different advice.

Or maybe we can bring together these contrasting commands by noticing what they have in common. In both cases, in Paul's directive to the Galatians and in his instruction to the Corinthians, Paul ultimately wants to restore the believer to the fellowship of the church. We see different methods to reach the same objective. Both cases seem to be based on a principle Paul discusses beginning in verse 6. The principle underlying Paul's strategy for dealing with immorality in the church is the assumption that Christianity and immorality do not mix. That is why the man's action is a travesty in the church at Corinth. That is why Paul suggests the plan of excommunication for the purpose of restoration. Christianity and immorality do not mix.

Why is that true? Why should we avoid immorality? Paul cites two reasons in our text. First, we should avoid immorality because of *how it affects others.* Note the question in verse 6: *Don't you know that a little leaven works through the whole batch of dough?* A little immorality in the life of one Christian can have a detrimental effect on the lives of other Christians. Second, we need to avoid immorality because of *who we are.*

Paul uses the metaphor of leavened and unleavened bread to remind the Corinthian Christians who they are. *Get rid of the old leaven that you may be a new batch without leaven—as you really are* (v. 7). Leaven is a substance added to dough to produce fermentation. In biblical literature the word takes on a figurative meaning as an additive that debases and corrupts the whole by a progressive inward infiltration. Because of the contaminating effect of leaven (in this case, representing the immorality of the man whose problem Paul addresses in our text), we should put away the leaven—that is, the immorality—so that we can begin living like the righteous men and women God declares us to be.

Christianity and immorality do not mix. That principle stands behind both Paul's instruction to the Corinthian Church and behind Paul's instruction to the Galatian church.

What does this passage mean for us today? Paul does not suggest isolating ourselves from the world so that the world's evil will not contaminate us. Paul's unambiguous response to such isolationism is seldom sounded in the evangelical world today, but it needs to be (vv. 9-10). Paul knows we cannot isolate ourselves from the immoral people in the world without getting out of the world, and that will defeat our purpose for being left in the world. Isolation from the world will undermine the framework of relationships essential for evangelism. We cannot isolate ourselves from the world.

Nor does Paul suggest that the church should expend all of its energy condemning the immorality of the world (v. 12). Many Christians today have become more public in their criticism of the immorality in the world, often targeting particular groups for harassment and public denunciation. They justify these actions by affirming, "The church must take a strong stand on moral issues." But taking a strong moral position in the world does not mean telling others what they should stand for as much as it means clearly demonstrating in our lives what we stand for. That is the thrust of Paul's questions in verse 12: *What business is it of mine to judge those outside the church? Are you not to judge those inside?* According to the passage, our business is not to judge those outside the church! Instead, we are to focus our attention on cleaning up our own act.

Nor does Paul advise kicking people out of the church whenever they do something wrong. Two reasons should caution us against wholesale church expulsions today. On the one hand, in today's world, if we kick a person out of the church, he or she can just go down the street and join another church. Excommunication today will not have the effect Paul wants to achieve by the strategy he suggests in our text. In addition, in a day when the world condemns the church because of our lack of compassion, kicking people out of the church will only feed that bad image among those who are not believers.

So what, then, does this passage mean for us today? I believe we should focus on the motive of Paul's appeal and the principle that stands behind it. Paul's *motive* is to restore those who are fallen. That motive provides the foundation for Paul's directive to the Corinthian church in our text. That motive also inspires Paul's advice in the Galatians passage. Out ultimate goal should be to strengthen every believer's relationship with God and to set straight in each other's lives the things that keep us from being the disciples Christ has called us and redeemed us to be. That motive may call for different methods in different churches just like Paul recommends different strategies to the churches at Corinth and Galatia. While the methods of dealing with the problem may change, the motive of restoration should remain constant.

Paul's *principle* at the foundation of this discussion is his conviction that Christianity and immorality do not mix. That principle lies behind Paul's advice to the Corinthians, and it also informs and shapes Paul's advice to the Galatians. This principle still applies today. Because of who we are and how immorality affects others, each of us needs to reaffirm our own decision to avoid immorality. The decision by each of us in the church to "be careful to do what is right in the eyes of everybody"—as Paul puts it in his Roman epistle (12:17)—is a giant step toward purifying the church. It will put us in a better position to carry out our responsibility of contextualizing the gospel of Jesus Christ in our community and in our world.

Note

1. Paul W. Powell, *The Complete Disciple* (Wheaton IL: Victor Books, 1982) 54.

15

The Church's Image

1 Corinthians 6:1-8

A little boy was running down the aisle of a grocery store when he slipped on some water that had dripped onto the floor from the vegetable section. The assistant manager, seeing what happened, rushed up to the little boy and said, "Don't cry. You'll be all right." The little boy replied, "I'm not going to cry. I'm going to sue!"

That is a common scene in our litigious society. Everybody is suing everybody. In Tulsa some time back, a construction worker used a circular saw to intentionally cut off one of his hands while on the work site. He claimed that the hand was possessed. Coworkers rushed the man to the hospital and brought the severed hand. At the hospital, the man demanded that the doctors not reattach the hand because it was possessed. Then, a few months later, he sued the doctors and hospital for damages because he claims they should have known that he was psychotic and reattached the hand anyway. Each of us can probably recall reading about some other ridiculous lawsuit. Instead of silently bearing our pain or releasing our emotion through tears, we are more likely to sue.

This litigious attitude also permeated the Roman world of Paul's day. The Roman court system had been established to deal with legitimate claims concerning breach of contract or fraud or personal injury. However, legitimate litigation soon gave way to vexatious litigation and many used the court system to settle scores with political opponents, to retaliate against an enemy, or to undercut someone who was more powerful. This litigious spirit also infects the citizens of Corinth, and in that litigious, vengeful city, Paul establishes a group of believers to whom he gives the responsibility to contextualize the gospel in their community so that they can begin to influence the city as the salt of the earth and the light of the world. But in this area as in other areas, the Corinthian Christians act more "Corinthian-like" than

"Christ-like." Like the pagan citizens of the city, the Corinthian Christians take each other to court in vexatious litigation. Paul addresses that problem in our text.

Some of the Corinthian Christians choose to take their lawsuits against fellow Christians to the pagan courts. Instead of settling their differences themselves, they present these disputes *before the ungodly for judgment* (v. 1). Some scholars suggest that the word "ungodly" refers to the character of the judges and that Paul therefore calls these judges corrupt or incompetent. Undoubtedly some incompetent judges did use the court system to enhance their own power and position, and a record from Corinth in about AD 90 alludes to "innumerable twisting judgments." Nevertheless, the word "ungodly" in our text probably means "nonbeliever" or "pagan." Paul does not imply that these judges will give unfair verdicts. He simply asserts that these judges are pagans. Yet Christians are calling in these pagan judges to settle their disagreements, which the judges are not qualified to do.

To emphasize the higher qualifications of those inside the church, Paul raises an intriguing question: *Do you not know that the saints will judge the world?* (v. 2). Both Matthew and Luke include a reference to Christians judging the world (Matt 19:28; Luke 22:29-30). Paul echoes those passages with this reference in his Corinthian epistle. Paul does not explain in what way the Corinthians will judge the world. Consequently, we should not become so bogged down in debating how Christians will judge the world that we miss Paul's point. Paul wants the Christians at Corinth to realize that believers qualified to *judge the world* (v. 2) should be able to take care of their own internal squabbles here on earth.

Embedded in this eschatological picture of judgment is another clue from Paul as to why the actions of these Corinthian Christians disturb him. Paul points out that the disagreements the Corinthian Christians take before the pagan judges to settle are *trivial cases* (v. 2). No one should take such trivial cases before an arbiter, and the Corinthian Christians should certainly not participate in such vexatious litigation.

Translators give different meanings to Paul's statement in verse 4. The New International Version translates this verse as an imperative: *Therefore, if you have disputes about such matters, appoint as judges even men of little account in the church*. In this case, Paul says something like this: "Even those you think are of 'little account in the church' can judge more wisely than the wise of the world." The New American Standard Bible translates this verse as a question: *If then you have law courts dealing with matters of this life, do you appoint them as judges who are of no account in the church?* In that case, Paul says something like this: "Why would you appoint someone *of little account to the church* to serve as judge over the disagreements among believers?" (v. 4).

Either translation makes the same point. The Corinthian Christians should not sue each other in the pagan courts. When they take their disagreements before the pagan courts instead of settling them themselves, Paul explains, they are *completely defeated already* (v. 7). Or, to express this truth in slightly different terms, by taking their disagreements before the pagan courts, they make the church fail to be the church.

How do the Corinthians fail to be the church? Let me offer two suggestions.

First of all, the Corinthian Christians *fail to be the church because they do not act as a community.* When Jesus prays for his disciples and for the church in his pastoral prayer on the final night of his life, he voices these words to God: "My prayer is not for them alone. I pray also for those who will believe in me through their message, that all of them may be one, Father, just as you are in me and I am in you" (John 17:20-21). Jesus prays for community. When Paul writes to the Ephesian church, divided as it is between those of Jewish background and those of Gentile background, he expresses his longing in these words: "For he himself is our peace, who has made the two one and has destroyed the barrier, the dividing wall of hostility, by abolishing in his flesh the law with its commandments and regulations. His purpose was to create in himself one new man out of the two, thus making peace" (Eph 2:14-15). Paul prays for community. The church is supposed to be one. We are united in Christ. We are family.

That view of the church arouses Paul's concern over the litigation between church members. Look at verses 5-6: *Is it possible that there is nobody among you wise enough to judge a dispute between believers? But instead, one brother goes to law against another.* Look at verses 7-8: *Why not rather be wronged? Why not rather be cheated? Instead, you yourselves cheat and do wrong, and you do this to your brothers.* Even the Roman legal system considers the family a sanctuary from enmity. And yet here are brothers and sisters in Christ who sue each other in the courts of the city. When they do this, they fail to act as the church, which is the family of God.

In addition, the Corinthian Christians *fail to be the church because they do not act as a witness.* Paul's concern about Christians taking other Christians to court also grows out of his desire for the church to present a positive image to the citizens of Corinth (vv. 3-7). Paul's statement in verse 7 provides the key to unlock the meaning of this passage. Paul writes, "It is surely obvious that something must be seriously wrong in your church for you to be having lawsuits at all" (Phillips). Obvious to whom? Paul suggests that the problem within the church is obvious to those in the world. If Christians who claim to be members of one family cannot get along, then obviously Christ does not make much of a difference in their lives. Consequently, instead of presenting to the world a positive image of the church, these Corinthian Christians present a negative image. Their failure to settle their internal squabbles within the church creates a bad image of the church in the city of Corinth and consequently neutralizes its witness to the world.

These two ideas emerge from our text: The Corinthian Christians do not act as a community. They do not present to the world a positive witness. Consequently, they fail to be the church.

This passage raises two key questions to ask about our churches today. Question 1 is this: *Do our churches act as a community?* Or, to put it in a slightly different way, *do we treat each other as family?*

In one of his books, Christian pollster George Barna reveals the result of his research on the family. He identifies some of the common characteristics of strong families.

- Strong, supportive, honest communication

- A significant quantity of time spent together

- Agreement on key values

- Love, consideration, understanding, and mutual appreciation

- Common interests, goals, and purposes

- Ability to negotiate solutions to crises positively

- Willingness to sacrifice personal interests and resources for the good of the family

- Behavior that earns the trust of family members (such as fidelity, loyalty, integrity)[1]

How many of these characteristics demonstrate the qualities of our church families? Do we major on building community?

Question 2 is this: *What kind of image do our churches have in the community?* In their book on the Buster generation, the generation of forty-six million Americans born between 1965 and 1980, Tim Celek and

Deiter Zander conclude, "When Busters look at the church, they see more roadblocks and detours than access points or paths to empowerment."[2]

What kind of image do our churches present to those who are on the outside? When nonbelievers look at our church, do they see roadblocks or access points?

A place of community for those who are in the family of God and a source of witness to those who are in the world—that is what a New Testament church is supposed to be. These conclusions about the church raise an important question: Do our churches act like a New Testament church? We must continually grapple with that question as we seek to contextualize the gospel in the communities around us.

Notes

1. George Barna, *The Future of the American Family* (Chicago: Moody Press, 1993) 205.

2. Tim Celek and Dieter Zander, *Inside the Soul of a New Generation* (Grand Rapids MI: Zondervan Publishing House, 1996) 91.

16

Right and Wrong

1 Corinthians 6:9–20

In a book a number of years ago, Christian intellectual Elton Trueblood suggested that the trouble in America today comes not from people breaking moral laws but from the conception that there are no moral laws to break, that there is no longer any distinction between right and wrong, that a person can thus do whatever he or she wants to do.[1] Signs of this amoral philosophy appear everywhere in our society today. In contrast to that amoral philosophy, the Bible clearly distinguishes between right and wrong. For example, our text for this chapter reminds us that as Christians, we are to commit ourselves to do what is right.

Paul makes that point in verse 11. After identifying the varieties of immorality rampant in Corinth, Paul adds, "But you were washed, you were sanctified, you were justified in the name of the Lord Jesus Christ and by the Spirit of our God." He then adds in verse 13 that the body is not meant for sexual immorality but for the Lord. Again, in verse 18, Paul declares, "Flee from sexual immorality." We have been sanctified—set apart—from the lifestyle of world. We have been called to live like Christ. We have been called to do what is right and not what is wrong. That message rings from our text, raising a practical question I want to consider in this chapter.

How can we determine what is right from what is wrong? Buddy Epsen, the actor who played the father on *The Beverly Hillbillies*, took a unique approach to morality. He said, "I simply ask myself if my mother would approve. If she wouldn't approve of some action, I don't do it."[2] That is not a bad plan. Former president Thomas Jefferson suggested this plan: "Ask how you would act if all the world were looking at you and act accordingly."[3] Charles Sheldon, in his classic book, *In His Steps*, suggested another plan for determining the right thing to do. Simply ask the question, "What would Jesus do if he were in my place?"[4]

Do we have a more specific plan, a set of principles we can call on when determining what is right and what is wrong? In our text for this chapter, Paul not only issues a call for morality. He also provides four principles to help us distinguish between right and wrong.

The first principle is the *holiness* principle (vv. 9-11). Note the question in verse 9: *Do you not know that the wicked will not inherit the kingdom of God?* Then observe the examples of unrighteous behavior provided. Paul mentions "the sexually immoral," those who participate in premarital sex; "idolaters," those who put something or someone else in the place rightly reserved for God; "adulterers," those who participate in sexual promiscuity with no regard for the marriage relationship; "male prostitutes," again referring to those who have no regard for the exclusiveness of the marriage relationship; "homosexual offenders," those who distort God's plan for sexual expression; "thieves," those who take what they want with no regard for private ownership; "the greedy," those who desire what belongs to others; "drunkards," those who engage in uncontrolled drunkenness; "slanderers," those who speak untrue and unkind words about others; and "swindlers," those who grasp that to which they have no right with a kind of savage ferocity. These people, Paul declares, "will not inherit the kingdom of God."

What does this mean? Paul does not mean that those who commit these sins are not Christians or never can be. Rather, he reminds the Christians at Corinth that they have been redeemed from these things. These things are not to be a part of the Christian lifestyle. The first step in determining right from wrong is to realize that some things are specifically prohibited in God's word, and these things are always wrong for the Christian

Where does the Bible identify these things? Our text provides one example. Paul specifically prohibits these nine things in the Christian life. We have been set apart from these things. We are not to do them.

We find another list in Exodus 20, the Ten Commandments. In calling his followers to a new righteousness, Jesus does not abolish the law. Instead, he calls his followers to a life that fulfills the original intention of the law. Consequently, we can assume that these things listed in the Ten Commandments are also prohibited from the Christian life.

Or we might consider the biblical admonition in Proverbs 6:16-19 to be another revelation of the things God proscribes from the lives of believers. The writer of Proverbs declares, "There are six things the Lord hates, seven that are detestable to him: haughty eyes, a lying tongue, hands that shed innocent blood, a heart that devises wicked schemes, feet that are quick to rush into evil, a false witness who pours out lies, and a man who stirs up dissension among brothers." In this numerical proverb, the first six items lead to and find their culmination in the seventh, "a man who stirs up dissension among brothers." God hates this, the Bible says. He always has and always will, and he does not want to see this kind of behavior in the lives of his children.

Throughout the epistles of Paul—for example, in Romans 1:28-32 and in Galatians 5:19-21—we find other lists of actions that are alien to the Christian lifestyle. Because of the life of holiness to which we have been called as Christians, we know some things are wrong for the Christian because God specifically says so in his word. That is the holiness principle.

A second principle is the *help* principle. There are some things not specifically restricted in God's word that Christians should nevertheless avoid because of Paul's suggestion in 1 Corinthians 6:12: *'Everything is permissible for me—but not everything is beneficial.* The New International Version puts quotation marks around the opening phrase in this verse: "Everything is permissible for me," suggesting that some of the Corinthians might have thrown this assertion at Paul, and he now counters this statement with his rejoinder: "But not everything is beneficial." Paul warns the Corinthians that although Christ has set them free, this does not allow them to do anything they want to do. Instead, they should only do those things that are good for them, that build them up as Christians, and that move them toward spiritual maturity.

Some live by the philosophy, "Eat, drink, and be merry, for tomorrow we may die." The problem with this philosophy is that we usually do not die the next day. Instead, we live to reap the consequences of our shortsighted pleasure. The inevitable connection between cause and effect is written into the moral framework of the universe. Because of that, Christians should avoid many things not specifically forbidden in God's word because of the consequences they bring in our lives and in the lives of others.

God's word does not specifically say, "Thou shalt not peruse a *Playboy* magazine or go to an X-rated movie." In that sense, we can conclude that these things are not unlawful. No specific biblical law prohibits them. Yet the realization that such activities will create unhealthy desires and clutter our minds with filth points to the conclusion that this activity is wrong for us as Christians.

As Christians we are to do things that build us up physically, mentally, and spiritually. Therefore, whenever we face a moral decision about which we have no specific statement in Scripture, we can ask ourselves this question: "Does this activity or event or relationship build me up? Is it good for me in the long run?" If the answer is no, then we should not do that thing. That is the help principle.

Paul presents a third principle still in verse 12, the *habit* principle. Paul declares, *Everything is permissible for me—but I will not be mastered by anything.* Again, in the opening phrase Paul probably quotes one of the Corinthian Christians and then responds in the second phrase. Some Corinthian Christians claim they have been set free in Christ. Paul counters with a reminder that even though they are free, they are not to be mastered by anything.

Paul's statement echoes an earlier declaration by Jesus in the Sermon on the Mount when he points out, "No one can serve two masters. Either he will hate the one and love the other, or he will be devoted to the one and despise the other" (Matt 6:24). As Christians, we cannot allow anything to control our lives except Jesus Christ himself. Because of that, some actions not specifically forbidden in God's Word are nevertheless wrong for us because they will ultimately control us. We will become addicted to them.

For example, the Bible does not say, "Thou shalt not smoke." This practice is not unlawful, but the realization of the dangers of becoming addicted to tobacco—and the evidence is incontrovertible—should cause Christians to conclude that this activity is wrong for us. Before we say "amen" to that example, we need to remember that this principle can also apply to those of us who cannot get started in the morning without our caffeine fix and those who cannot go to bed at night without a Twinkie carefully balanced on a mound of Blue Bell ice cream. Paul admonishes us not to become addicted to anything. Consequently, when we are faced with a decision or tempted by an action, we should consider whether this decision or this action will push us down the pathway of dependency. If it will, then this decision or action is wrong for us as Christians, and we should not do it. That is the habit principle.

We find a fourth principle in the final verse of the chapter. We might call it the honor principle. Paul writes, "You were bought at a price. Therefore honor God with your body" (6:20). Paul provides a fuller expression of this principle later in his letter to the Corinthians when he writes, "So whether you eat or drink or whatever you do, do it all for the glory of God" (1 Cor 10:31). We are to glorify God in everything we do. Therefore, some activities are wrong for the Christian, even if they are not specifically forbidden, even if they are not bad for us, and even if they are not habit forming simply because they do not honor God. If we are serious about doing what is right as a Christian, then before we do something, we should ask, "Will this activity make God look good? Will this activity enhance God's reputation?" If not, then we should not participate in that activity. That is the honor principle.

So here are the four principles to help us determine right from wrong:

- The holiness principle—what does God's word say about it?

- The help principle—will this be good for me?

- The habit principle—will this become habit forming?

- The honor principle—will this make God look good?

Notes

1. Elton Trueblood, *A Place to Stand* (New York: Harper & Row, 1969) 16.
2. *Pensacola News-Journal TV Tabs*, 15 July 1979, 7.
3. *Quote* 72/16 (17 October 1976): 371.
4. Charles Sheldon, *In His Steps* (Ulrichsville OH: Barbour Publishing Co., 2005).

17

Christian Marriage

1 Corinthians 7:1-16

A woman hired a lawyer to discuss her desire for a divorce. The lawyer said, "You need to realize this is one of the most painful actions a person can take. You need to be sure about it. So I want to ask you this question: Do you have any grounds for divorce?" "Well," the woman replied, "I guess we have ten acres with a swimming pool." "No," the lawyer responded. "I don't think you understand. What I mean is, do you have a grudge?" The potential client answered, "Well, we actually have a three-car garage—one for his Mercedes, one for my Lexus, and one for the truck." Shaking his head, the lawyer mumbled, "I still don't think I'm getting through. Let me try this question: Does your husband ever beat you up?" "Oh, no," the wife answered, "I always get up at six o'clock to fix the coffee but he never gets up until at least seven o'clock." The exasperated lawyer finally shouted, "What I'm trying to find out is why you want a divorce!" The woman responded, "Well, my husband tells me we have this problem communicating!" Oh, really?

Communication problems often plague marriages, in the first century and in our century, but learning how to communicate effectively is only one of the many challenges in the relationship called marriage. Even though God established marriage in the beginning and even though marriage is God's idea, because we live in a fallen world, living up to God's ideal for marriage is not always easy. As one old quip put it, "Marriages might be made in heaven, but they have to be lived out down here on earth." Ironically, just being a person of faith does not solve the problems of marriage. Sometimes our faith leads us to decisions that actually increase the level of conflict in the home.

We see this dilemma in the Corinthian church. Paul takes the gospel of Jesus Christ to the immoral, pagan, urban center of the ancient world called Corinth and leaves behind a community of believers. As Christians, God has called them to a new life in Christ. But what does that new life look like, and how does it affect their old life? The Corinthian Christians confront those questions, and some of them relate specifically to marriage. Paul responds to the questions about marriage in this seventh chapter of his Corinthian letter.

Let me give a brief overview of the kinds of questions the Corinthians ask about marriage and a summary of Paul's responses. The unmarried Corinthians want to know if it is all right to get married as a Christian or whether they should remain single. Paul suggests either marriage or singleness as a viable choice for Christians. The married Corinthians want to know if the sexual dimension of marriage is evil and therefore to be avoided. Paul affirms that it is not. The Corinthian Christians married to believers want to know if they should stay married or separate. Paul tells them to stay together. The Corinthian Christians married to unbelievers want to know if they should leave their pagan spouses. Paul tells them to stay together if the unbelieving partner agrees to it. The Corinthian Christians married to unbelievers who want to leave them wonder if they should fight to save their marriages. Paul advises, "Let them go."

These questions and answers evolve from a number of issues that arise in the context of the first-century city of Corinth as Christians try to contextualize the gospel in that pagan city. In 1 Corinthians 7:1-16, which is our text for this chapter, Paul responds to two of these questions. In each case, we see the issue, Paul's response to that issue, and the underlying principle that provides the foundation for Paul's response.

The first *issue* relates to the Christian's response to the sexual dimension of marriage (vv. 2-9). Remembering the context of the Corinthian church will illuminate why the Corinthians struggle with this issue. Sexuality permeates the city of Corinth in the first century. Immorality weaves through the fabric of the city. Even worse, the established religions of the city actually sanction sexuality with their "priestesses of vice" who ply their trade in the temple to Aphrodite, the goddess of love. We might say sex has a bad reputation in the city of Corinth, for it is inextricably connected with both immorality and idolatry.

As a result, when these Corinthians become Christians, they wonder if the sexual dimension of life is now taboo for them. If sex is immoral and if the idolatrous practices in the city highlight this casual sexuality, then maybe they should give up this part of married life altogether. Some of the Corinthian Christians opt for total abstinence. The statement in the opening verse of our text—which is more accurately translated "It is good for a man not to touch a woman"—captures the approach of some of the new Christians at Corinth.

Paul's *response* takes a different tack. Of course you can participate in sex within marriage, Paul declares. Sexual intimacy is a natural part of life, and God has designed marriage as the proper context for the full expression of our sexuality. To refuse this part of married life distorts the proper relationship between a husband and wife. Paul affirms that marriage provides the proper arena for the expression of human sexuality.

Paul's response grows out of the underlying *principle* of marriage as a partnership. This passage is not primarily about sexuality. It focuses instead on the nature of marriage. That is why Paul surmises in verse 4, *The wife's body does not belong to her alone but also to her husband. In the same way, the husband's body does not belong to him alone but also to his wife.* When we get married, we become a part of a relationship in which our body is no longer our own, and the word "body" does not just mean our physical body but our whole self. What we do with our body, how we express our desires, how we in fact live out our lives are no longer issues for us to decide alone. Rather, they are issues we are to decide together as husband and wife. Marriage is a partnership.

We see no hint here of wives submitting to their husbands but rather husbands and wives mutually submitting to each other as equal partners. Marriage is a partnership. In verse 5, where Paul allows abstinence from the sexual relationships in marriage for a season, this is not to be done at the arbitrary command of the husband or the solo decision of the wife. Instead, it is to be made mutually between husband and wife. Marriage is a partnership. Paul presents that idea as the first principle of marriage.

A secondary *issue* facing the Corinthian Christians has to do with their response to change (vv. 10-16). Remember what has happened to these Corinthians who have become believers. Their decision to become Christians has turned their whole world upside down. Instead of wallowing in the immorality of that day, they are called to a new life of purity. Instead of seeking their own will, they are called to seek God's will. Instead of living only for today, they are to live for eternity. Instead of participating in the debauchery of idol worship, they are to worship the one true God. Their whole world has been turned upside down.

How should they respond to these changes? Should they give up on their marriages so they can serve God more fully? Should they send their unbelieving spouses away so they can give their attention fully to Christ? That is the issue. Some of the Corinthian Christians apparently opt for separation. Because they believe that being married to a pagan will defile them in some way, they conclude that divorcing a pagan spouse is their Christian duty.

Paul's *response* discards the idea of separation and instead urges married couples to stay together, even if one of the partners is not a believer. Paul does not want them to give up on marriage, nor does he want them to send their unbelieving spouses away. Instead, they should remain married, for Christian believers can perhaps influence their unbelieving spouses to become Christians. Likewise, Christian parents can create an environment in the home in which the children can come to a decision about Christ. Paul affirms that leaving an unbelieving spouse is not a sign of superior spirituality. The spiritual thing for the Corinthian Christians to do is to stay married and to sanctify their homes with their Christian living.

Paul's response grows out of the underlying *principle* that marriage is to be permanent. This passage is not just about changing circumstances. It is also about the unchanging nature of marriage. That is why Paul explains in verses 10-11, *To the married I give this command (not I, but the Lord): A wife must not separate from her husband. But if she does, she must remain unmarried or else be reconciled to her husband. And a husband must not divorce his wife.* When we get married, we become a part of a relationship that is not to be broken. Marriage is to be permanent. No matter what changing circumstances arise, we are not to use our faith as an excuse to terminate a relationship that has been affected by these circumstances. Marriage is to be permanent.

We see two issues, two responses, and two principles at the foundation: marriage is a partnership, and marriage is to be permanent.

How are we to respond to these principles? I think we have three options.

First, *we can view these principles as irrelevant to today's world and discard them.* Whether it is the serious expression of an article in the *Atlantic* magazine where the author asserts, "Without the sacrament of Divorce, who would be silly enough to get married?"[1] or the frivolous statement of a Hollywood celebrity who justified the elaborate plans for her marriage with the comment, "I want this to be a nice affair. After all, marriage is something you only do four or five times in your lifetime," many see marriage as a temporary relationship to retain as long as it is convenient but to discard when it becomes uncomfortable. That is not the biblical view nor should it be the opinion of those who follow Christ.

The second option is that *we can view these principles as unassailable laws and enforce them.* We can consider no exceptions and no grace and no understanding of the fallenness of our world—just a rigid, legalistic application of the principles that justifies our condemnation of those who do not live up to them. Some people take this position regarding the principles of marriage.

Again, I do not think this is the biblical view, nor should it be the position of those who follow Christ.

A third position is to *view these principles as best practices and live by them*. This avoids the unprincipled approach of those who discard these biblical truths, but it also avoids the legalistic approach of those who are long on judgment and short on grace. Tony Campolo expresses this approach in his book, *The Success Fantasy*: "I think the church is obligated to accept the difficult challenge of upholding a principle, on the one hand, and being gracious to the violators, on the other. This is extremely difficult, because graciousness to violators can easily be interpreted as laxity concerning the principle. The church must stand opposed to divorce, yet remain accepting and open toward those who violate the principle."[2] That seems to be the Christian approach.

Yet even in a fallen world we need to affirm this truth continually: God wants husbands and wives to come together in permanent partnerships that bring fulfillment to those in the family and that bring honor to God. May we ever commit ourselves to that biblical principle.

Notes

1. *Quote* 71/21 (23 May 1976): 485.

2. Anthony Campolo, *The Success Fantasy* (Wheaton IL: Victor Books, 1980) 122.

18

Remain As You Are

1 Corinthians 7:17–24

We can hardly miss the central message in our text for this chapter because Paul repeats his theme three times. He begins the passage with his theme in verse 17: *Nevertheless, each one should retain the place in life that the Lord assigned to him.* He repeats it in verse 20: *Each one should remain in the situation which he was in when God called him.* He then ends the passage with the theme in verse 24: *Brothers, each man, as responsible to God, should remain in the situation God called him to.* No mystery clouds Paul's intention in this passage. He reminds the Corinthian Christians of their situation when God called them to a new life in Christ. Paul then instructs them, *Remain as you are.*

What does Paul mean by that statement? Based on a number of comments the Apostle Paul makes in his other epistles, we can conclude that he does not instruct the Corinthians not to grow as Christians. He does not tell them they should stay at the same spiritual level. For example, Paul calls on the Roman Christians to develop spiritually. "Do not conform any longer to the pattern of this world," he writes, "but be transformed by the renewing of your mind" (Rom 12:2). He challenges the Ephesian Christians to develop spiritually. "Speaking the truth in love," he writes, "we will in all things grow up into him who is the Head, that is, Christ" (Eph 4:15). He reminds the Philippian Christians that he has committed himself to grow spiritually. "Not that I have already obtained all this, or have already been made perfect," he writes, "but I press on to take hold of that for which Christ Jesus took hold of me" (Phil 3:12). In fact, every image of the Christian life in the New Testament assumes growth and development: a baby who needs to grow up, a race that needs to be run, a journey that needs to be taken, and a house that needs to be built. So when Paul says to the Corinthian Christians, "Remain as you are," he obviously does not mean they should be satisfied at whatever spiritual level they find themselves.

What then does Paul mean when he tells the Corinthian Christians, not once but three times in this short passage, *Each one should remain in the situation which he was in when God called him* (v. 20)? Paul wants them to know that the call to Christ transcends all other circumstances of their lives and thus makes these circumstances irrelevant.

In the larger passage of 1 Corinthians 7, Paul has already illustrated that truth in relationship to marriage. Whether or not Christians are married has nothing to do with their spirituality. A single person can be a Christian, and a married person can also be a Christian. The call to Christ transcends our marital status and makes it irrelevant spiritually. Paul now illustrates that truth in two other areas.

In verses 18-19, Paul applies this truth to a person's *ethnic identity*. To the first-century Jews, two groups of people populate the earth: the Jews and everyone else, the Jews and the Gentiles. Circumcision serves as the mark that separates the Jews from the Gentiles. Paul, who has been born and bred in the Jewish culture, knows that as well as anyone. As he points out in Philippians 3:4-6, his Jewish credentials are unimpeachable. Because of that, Paul's statement in verse 19 is certainly one of the most radical things Paul ever said: *Circumcision is nothing.* How can a Jewish man raised in the Jewish culture, a Pharisee of the Pharisees, make such a radical statement? The source out of which this remarkable statement comes is Paul's conviction, repeated three times in our text, that the call to Christ transcends all the other circumstances of our lives and makes them irrelevant.

In verses 21-23, Paul applies this truth to a person's *social standing*. To catch the spirit of Paul's contrast between those who are slaves and those who are free, we should not conjure up the picture of a Southern plantation in Georgia in the middle of the nineteenth century. Instead, think of the class distinctions that divided English society just a few generations back. For example, I recently watched the remarkable saga based on Barbara Taylor Bradford's novel *A Woman of Substance*. The story revolves around a young servant girl, Emma Harte, who overcomes every imaginable circumstance to become one of the richest women in the world. The early part of the story revolves around a romance between her and the young son of the master of the house. When the cook sees this romance beginning to develop, she pulls Emma aside and warns her, "This will never work. You can't get out of your class. Whenever you try to rise out of your class, you will only get hurt."

That mindset provides the context for Paul's statement in our text. Paul has in mind the idea of distinct classes in society, each class operating at a different level. Conventional wisdom in his day suggests that whenever people try to get out of their class, they are headed for trouble. That idea permeates the society of Paul's day. It's a society with clear demarcations between different social levels in which no one dares to move out of his or her class. Paul is very much aware of those ingrained social standards.

Why would someone in that clearly layered society make such a radical statement as Paul makes in verse 22? *For he who was a slave when he was called by the Lord is the Lord's freedman,* he writes. *Similarly, he who was a free man when he was called is Christ's slave.* Again, the source out of which this remarkable statement comes is Paul's conviction, repeated three times, that the call to Christ transcends all the other circumstances of our lives and makes them irrelevant.

Remain as you are, Paul tells the Corinthian Christians, encouraging them to focus on the call of Christ.

How does this truth from Paul intersect with our lives today as we try to contextualize the gospel in our urban and global environment? The fact that our call to Christ transcends all the circumstances of our lives and makes them irrelevant takes away any excuses we might have for not living for Christ each day.

We regularly hide behind such excuses. We say, "I can't live for Christ because . . . ," and then we list some circumstance in our lives. I'm too young. I'm too old. I have too much responsibility. No one ever gives me any responsibility. I was deprived in my childhood. I was pampered in my childhood. We have an endless list of circumstances we can use to explain lack of commitment.

I heard about a man who once said, "If I had some extra money, I'd give it to God, but I have just enough to support myself and my family." The same man said, "If I had some extra time, I'd give it to God, but every minute is taken up with my job, my family, my clubs—every single minute." He also said, "If I had a talent, I'd give it to God, but I have no lovely voice; I have no special skill; I've never been able to lead a group; I can't think cleverly or quickly the way I would like to." God was touched by the man's condition, so he gave that man money, time, and a glorious talent. Then God waited and waited and waited. After a while, God shrugged his shoulders and took all those things back from the man: the money, the time, and the glorious talent. After a while the man sighed and said, "If I only had some of that money back, I'd give it to God. If I only had some of that time, I'd give it to God. If I could only rediscover that glorious talent, I'd give it to God." The list of circumstances we can use to explain why we are not living for Christ is endless.

Sometimes we project our service to God into the future and say, "Someday, when I get certain things taken care of, then I will serve Christ." One person expressed this truth in these poignant words:

> First I was dying to finish high school and start college.
> And then I was dying to finish college and start working.
> And then I was dying to marry and have children.
> And then I was dying for my children to grow old enough for school so I could return to work.
> And then I was dying to retire.
> And now, I am dying . . . and suddenly I realize I forgot to live."[1]

Some Christians consistently project their service for Christ into the future and make the promise that when the circumstances get exactly right, then they will serve Christ.

Paul reminds us in our text that the call to Christ that transcends all our circumstances and makes them irrelevant takes away our excuses with the reminder that every one of us, right now, right here, with what we have, can serve the living Christ and make a contribution to his kingdom.

In his famous "I Have a Dream" speech, Martin Luther King, Jr., said, "We have come to this hallowed spot to remind America of the fierce urgency of now."[2] Paul makes precisely that point in our text. Paul calls the Christians of Corinth in the first century and those of us who claim to be believers in the twenty-first century to live out our Christian lives in the fierce urgency of now.

In the fierce urgency of now, what are we doing to build up the kingdom of God? To whom are we talking about the Lord? How are we ministering to people? We do not have to become another person. We do not have to develop different gifts. We do not have to go somewhere else. We do not have to grow up or slow down or go to work or retire or marry or get a degree or learn more about the Bible. Right now, right here, with what we have, every one of us can serve the living Christ and make a contribution to his kingdom. The question is, will we do it?

Notes

1. Barbara De Angelis, *Real Moments* (New York: Dell Publishing, 1994) 3.
2. Paul W. Powell, *The Night Cometh* (Tyler TX: Self-published, 2002) 9.

19

You Don't Have to Be Married to Serve God

1 Corinthians 7:25-40

An eight-year-old boy reluctantly attended summer camp for the first time in his life. His first letter to his mother went like this: "Dear Mom, I told you something terrible would happen if I went off to camp. Well, it did. Sincerely, Joe."

When Paul received correspondence from the Christians at Corinth, he might have been gripped by the same uneasy feeling as that mother. These Christians are his children in the faith, whom he brought into the kingdom and carefully instructed. Yet terrible things seem to be happening to them. Problems erupt on every hand. Confusion leads to division. They need help. So they write to Paul for advice about their problems.

One of the problems disturbing them has to do with the choice between remaining single or getting married. The Corinthian Christians want to know if it is really a sin to get married or is it a sin to remain single. Chapter 7 of Paul's first Corinthian epistle answers those questions.

What advice does Paul give the Corinthian Christians? To begin with, he reminds them that marriage is a permanent partnership (7:1-16). Then he reminds them that the call to Christ transcends all the circumstances of their lives and makes them irrelevant (7:17-24). Therefore, they can serve God in his kingdom work whatever their circumstances. We have explored those responses in the two previous chapters. But we need to notice another message that weaves its way through Paul's advice in the first section of this chapter and comes into focus in the remaining verses of the chapter. Paul wants the Corinthian Christians to realize that a person does not have to be married to serve God.

Notice how Paul highlights that theme. In verse 7 he writes, "I wish that all men were as I am"—that is, single. In verse 8 he adds, "Now to the unmarried and the widows I say: It is good for them to stay unmarried, as I am." He echoes the same theme in verses 25-26: *Now about virgins: I have no command from the Lord, but I give a judgment as one who by the Lord's mercy is trustworthy. Because of the present crisis, I think that it is good for you to remain as you are.* Then he adds in verse 40, addressing the widow, *In my judgment, she is happier if she stays as she is.* Finally, in the most extended statement on this theme he declares,

> An unmarried man is concerned about the Lord's affairs—how he can please the Lord. But a married man is concerned about the affairs of this world—how he can please his wife—and his interests are divided. . . . I am saying this for your own good, not to restrict you, but that you may live in a right way in undivided devotion to the Lord. (vv. 32-35)

In each of these passages Paul affirms that being single does not restrict Christian service. A person can be single and still be spiritual. A person can be single and still be in the center of God's will. A person can be single and still serve God.

While that declaration might not be startling to us today, it shocked many in Paul's day. No culture in Paul's time favored the idea of celibacy or singleness. In the Old Testament Jewish world, marriage is almost universal. The only ones not married are those who through physical damage, either accidental or purposeful, are unable to perform sexually. Spinsters do not exist. The Old Testament does not even mention a word for "bachelor." Widows exist, of course, but the law of Levirate marriage provides a means by which these widows can become married again. A widow not claimed by a brother of her ex-husband or reclaimed by her own family often lives in disgrace. Some scholars even suggest that widows have to wear special garments to identify themselves as widows.

The same feeling carried over into the New Testament period. The first-century Jews expect everyone to marry. William Barclay tells of an early Jewish document that mentions seven types of persons who will be excommunicated from heaven, and the list begins, "A Jew who has no wife . . . ." First-century citizens consider marriage to be the normal state of life. Indeed, that idea prevails in almost every culture of that day. Yet in that context, Paul pronounces this radical idea: being single is an acceptable status for the Christian. A person can be single and still be in the middle of God's will. In fact, because marriage divides our interests, Paul claims that in many ways we can develop our personal devotion to God more as a single than if we are married.

The early church picks up this theme from Paul, and many church fathers in the first three centuries either practice or praise the single life. By the year AD 300, in the Council of Elvira, a local Spanish council imposed celibacy for the first time on the bishops of that area. Gradually, celibacy became the imposed pattern for all priests and bishops of the church. Singleness came to be exalted as the highest state for a Christian.

A radical reaction to that idea grew out of the Reformation period. Celibacy again lost favor and marriage was exalted once more as the highest state for a Christian relationship. We are still living in the aftermath of the Reformation thinking. We too often attach a stigma to singleness. For example, when I graduated from Baylor, a friend of mine who had graduated from seminary could not get a church to call him as pastor because he was single. He was a good preacher and adequately prepared for the ministry—all dressed up with nowhere to go. Why? He had simply chosen at that point not to be married. We sometimes unconsciously promote in our churches the idea that singleness is undesirable.

In that kind of situation, we need to affirm again the often forgotten alternative of singleness. We need to announce with the Apostle Paul that a person does not have to be married to serve God. We need to affirm that single adults can find their place in the family of God. How does this affirmation affect us as we do kingdom work today?

The challenge of this affirmation comes first of all to the church. Based on this affirmation in our text, every church today needs to affirm the worth of single adults. A person's worth does not come simply in the person to whom he or she is married. A person's worth is not found simply in the children that person may produce. A person's worth is found in the person he or she is and in that person's relationship with God. We need to remind single adults of their value and importance to God.

Then we need to offer opportunities for single adults to find companionship with integrity. When God says, "It is not good for the man to be alone" (Gen 2:18), he affirms a basic truth about humanity. We all need companionship. If we do not find that companionship with a husband or a wife, we need to find it in friends and colleagues. It is not good to be alone, for loneliness is a terribly frightening experience. However, many of the places where single adults can find companionship come loaded with temptation and danger. We need to provide opportunities for single adults to find friends, enjoy companionship, and develop relationships and still maintain their integrity.

We also need to provide opportunities for single adults to serve the Lord in our churches. Paul implies in our text that the interests of single adults are not as divided. That means single adults might have more opportunity and more time to express their devotion to God than those who are married. Single adults not only have the opportunity to serve but also have the gifts to serve. Consequently, we need to become churches in which singles can have their worth affirmed, their companionship needs met, and opportunities to use their gifts of God in ministry in the church.

But Paul also has a challenge for those who are single. First, Paul's affirmation in our text challenges single adult Christians to identify with the body of Christ. Some single adults like to keep their options open and want to remain free of any kind of entanglements. Sometimes they even use their singleness as an excuse for not getting involved in the church. But Christian singles have a responsibility to plant their lives in a local New Testament church where God can use them to carry out his kingdom work.

Paul's affirmation in our text also challenges single adults to become involved in kingdom work. I have had the privilege throughout my ministry to work with single adults, both in the churches where I have served and in national and state conferences for single adults where I have spoken. On many occasions I have heard the sad tale of single adults who want to get involved in God's work, who want to be in the church too, but who are discouraged by churches that will not accept them or by pastors who will not work with them. We should counter that tendency and provide a loving and accepting community where single adults can be involved in service to God's kingdom.

Paul's affirmation in our text also calls single adults to integrity. Single adults cannot use their circumstances in life, their singleness, as an excuse for being anything else or anything less than what God wants them to be. The important issues are whether we are committed to God's will, walking in God's way, and living by God's word. Some singles might try to excuse their inactivity or indifference by declaring, "I am single. I really do not have anything to give." On the contrary, Paul sends out this word to the single adults in both the first century and in the twenty-first century. God has called you and equipped you to help in contextualizing the gospel in the pluralistic and global context of the twenty-first century.

Note

1. William Barclay, *The Letter to the Corinthians*, rev. ed. (Philadelphia: The Westminster Press, 1975) 61.

20

Christians Who Are Christian

1 Corinthians 8:1-6

Several years ago a Canadian writer, Wilfred Cantwell Smith, wrote *Questions of Religious Truth*. The final chapter in this book is titled "Christian—Noun or Adjective." Dr. Smith says that if someone asks him if he is a Christian, he will readily answer, "Yes," for at a specific moment in his life he made a commitment to Christ and became a Christian. That is, he uses "Christian" as a noun. Dr. Smith goes on to say that if someone asks him if he is Christian, using the term as an adjective, the situation changes dramatically. This question, admits Dr. Smith—using the term "Christian" as an adjective—is a disturbing, probing question that is not so easy to answer.[1]

I know exactly how he feels. Christian as a noun? Those of us who have professed our faith in Jesus will affirm it without hesitation. But Christian as an adjective—that is, claiming that we live each day authentically and consistently in a Christian way? We might not affirm this so quickly.

Like Christians of every century, the first-century Christians at Corinth have to deal with this distinction. On his second missionary journey, Paul stops in Corinth. According to Acts 18, Paul first shares the message about Jesus in the Jewish synagogue. Then, when some of the Jews oppose Paul's teaching, he leaves the synagogue and goes next door to the house of a God-fearer named Titius Justis. By "God-fearer," Luke means a spiritually sensitive Gentile drawn to the teachings of Judaism. For an extended time, Paul continues to preach the gospel of Christ and call people to put their faith in Jesus. Many respond, both Jews and Gentiles, so that when Paul leaves Corinth he has established a church there, leaving behind men and women who have put their faith in Jesus Christ and who now must live as Christians in the pagan city of Corinth. These Corinthian Christians do not question the validity of their relationship with Christ. They know they are Christians, using that word as a noun. The challenging issue is how to live in the pagan city of Corinth in a Christian way. In other words, they struggle with being Christian, using that word as an adjective. First Corinthians is Paul's attempt to help them understand how to be Christian in the city of Corinth.

This challenge becomes particularly difficult when the Corinthian Christians have to decide what to do about the food sacrificed to idols. Citizens of ancient Corinth regularly offer sacrifices to the various gods, both in the pagan temples and in the homes of the people. Some of the food they offer as a sacrifice in a pagan temple ends up being served in social gatherings or sold on the open market. Some of the food they offer as a sacrifice in the home is used as the main course for a banquet or celebration feast. These common practices present a dilemma for the Corinthian Christians. If they buy meat at these pagan temples or on the open market, or if they participate in meals in the homes of pagans, they might be purchasing or eating meat that has been offered to idols.

Some of the Corinthian Christians think this meat is tainted by the idols and refuse to eat it. Others consider these idols to be empty symbols meaning nothing. So they feel they can eat this meat without fear. The Corinthian Christians cannot reach a consensus in the church, so they raise the question with Paul: what is the Christian thing to do?

Before we look at Paul's instruction to the Corinthian Christians, let me pause to deal with a question that might have come to your mind as you read this: what does this have to do with us today? To be sure, we do not debate today about whether or not to eat food sacrificed to idols, and we do not have to worry about whether or not the meat we buy at the marketplace is spiritually tainted. So what does this passage of Scripture have to do with us? The struggles facing the Corinthians differ from our struggles today, yet the underlying issue is the same. In the daily decisions of our lives, how can we determine the Christian thing to do? That is the deeper issue Paul addresses our text, and that issue is certainly relevant to each of us as Christians today.

What is the Christian thing to do in relationship to the food offered to idols? We find the essence of Paul's instruction in verse 1: *Now about food sacrificed to idols: we know that we all possess knowledge. Knowledge puffs up, but love builds up.* In determining whether or not to eat the food sacrificed to idols, the Corinthian Christians can choose one of two options. They can act on the basis of what they know, or they can act on the basis of how their actions will affect other Christians. Knowledge or love—they have to choose between these two alternative motivations.

Apparently, some in the Corinthian church believe *knowledge* is the key factor in determining their actions. *We know an idol is nothing at all in the world and that there is no God but one* (v. 4). When Paul makes that statement, he seems to be quoting someone in the Corinthian church. "We know there is only one god," they assert. "This meat is not contaminated because these other gods do not even exist. They are just a figment of the imagination, and we know it. If the other Christians cannot figure that out, then that is their problem. We are going to act on the basis of what we know and let the chips fall where they may."

Many in the Corinthian church opted for knowledge as their primary motivation. In contrast, Paul suggests that *love* should be the key factor in determining our actions. Knowledge says we will do whatever we think is right, but love says we will not do anything that will cause other Christians to stumble. Paul challenges the Christians at Corinth to determine their actions not by knowledge but by love, not by what they want to do but by how their actions will affect others.

Now before we apply this principle to our lives, let me make one point of clarification. Paul does not say that everything we do is to be determined by what other people think. The unanimous testimony of Scripture is against such an approach.

Look at Jesus' life, for instance. Jesus confronts a man with a withered hand on the Sabbath. The religious leaders demand that he do nothing. Instead, Jesus heals the man (Matt 12:9-14). Rabbis of Jesus' day do not associate with publicans and known sinners. To do so would be to defile oneself and call one's commitment into question. Yet Jesus becomes so closely associated with the sinners of his day and has such close fellowship with them that his enemies call him "a glutton and a drunkard" (Luke 7:34). When Jesus announces to his disciples that he will die, Peter, probably speaking for the entire group, rebukes him. He protests, "Master, we don't want you to do it" (Matt 16:22, author's paraphrase). But Jesus goes to the cross anyway. The opinions and wishes of others do not motivate Jesus. Rather, he marches to the drumbeat of the will of God. "Yet not my will but yours be done" (Luke 22:42) is the theme that shapes Jesus' choices.

We see the same response in the early disciples. Their peers do not determine their actions. Rather, they act according to the principle Peter and John voice in Acts 4:20: "For we cannot help speaking about what we have seen and heard."

How then can we reconcile the actions of Jesus and the disciples and Paul with what Paul says to the Corinthian Christians in our text? Are we to determine our actions by what others think or not? Paul's statement in verse 8 provides the key. Paul declares, *But food does not bring us near to God; we are no worse if we do not eat, and no better if we do.* The act of eating the meat is neither good nor bad in and of itself. Eating meat will not draw us closer to God nor drive us further away from God. It is morally neutral. In matters that are morally neutral, when our action will neither especially help us nor harm us, we are to be primarily motivated by the influence of this action on the lives of others.

On the other hand, some actions are not morally neutral. Some actions are right and always right. These we must do regardless of what others may think. Identifying with God's cause—that is always right. Helping people who are in need—that is always right. Valuing every person as a person of worth—that is always right. Standing up for the truth—that is always right. Keeping ourselves pure—that is always right. Sharing the gospel with those who are lost—that is always right. We cannot use this passage as an excuse to keep from doing the things we know we as Christians ought to do just because someone else might not like it.

Having noted the exception, let me repeat now the principle Paul presents in this chapter. In areas that are morally neutral, our responsibility as Christians is to do the most loving thing. When I say "love," I am not talking about some soft and sentimental emotion. I am not talking about the human love that responds to what is appealing and lasts as long as it is rewarded. I am talking about the kind of Christian love that, in every situation, asks the question, "What will be the best thing for this particular person?" I am talking about the kind of Christian love that breaks us free of our self-absorbed question, "What's in it for me?" and asks instead, "How will this affect the other person?" That is a true description of Christian love.

If, at the end of each day, we can give an affirmative answer to the question, "Have I loved today?" then we will know we are not only Christians, using that term as a noun, but also Christian, using that term as an adjective. After all, Jesus Christ himself once said, "They will know we are Christian by our love" (John 13:35).

Note

1. J. A Davidson, "'Christian': Noun or Adjective," *Pulpit Digest 63/462* (July/August 1983): 18.

21

The Myth of Unlimited Freedom

1 Corinthians 8:7-13

As we live our lives, we often determine our actions on the basis of what we call "old wives' tales." Old wives' tales are superstitious stories that predict inevitable results from certain actions. Some of these tales are common, and probably most of us are familiar with them: it is bad luck to leave a house through a different door than the one used to come into it, an apple a day keeps the doctor away, if we blow out all the candles on our birthday cake with the first puff we will get our wish, or breaking a mirror means seven years of bad luck. Other old wives' tales are perhaps not so well known, at least to me, like this one I ran across recently: to cure a cough, take a hair from the coughing person's head, put it between two slices of buttered bread, feed it to a dog, and say, "Eat well, you hound, may you be sick and I be sound." Most of these superstitious tales are harmless, and believing them will hardly affect our lives. On the other hand, other myths are not so innocuous. Following these myths will push our lives in the wrong direction and harm the world around us.

I want us to consider a dangerous kind of myth in this chapter: the myth of unlimited freedom. The myth goes something like this: because we have been set free in Jesus Christ, we can do whatever we want to do, regardless of what others think and regardless of how our actions affect the lives of others.

To be sure, the New Testament repeatedly announces our freedom in Christ. For instance, in his second Corinthian epistle, Paul asserts, "Now the Lord is the Spirit, and where the Spirit of the Lord is, there is freedom" (2 Cor 3:17). To the Galatians Paul declares, "It is for freedom that Christ has set us free" (Gal 5:1). He then adds, a few verses later, "You, my brothers, were called to be free" (Gal 5:13). To the Ephesians Paul affirms, "In him and through faith in him we may approach God with freedom and confidence" (Eph 3:12). Freedom in Christ is one of the central themes of the New Testament. One of the most beautiful New Testament images of Jesus' redemptive work grows out of the slave market. We stand in bondage because of our sin, but Jesus pays the ransom to set us free. The theme of freedom in Christ permeates the New Testament.

The desire for freedom also pulsates through humanity in every generation in human history and in every age. This desire for freedom begins at an early age when two-year-olds add to their vocabulary the word, "No!" It is reflected in the lives of teenagers who rebel against both family and societal rules and regulations. We see it in college students who complain to the teacher, "Why are you giving us this assignment? It has absolutely nothing to do with my life." Adults demonstrate it when they flagrantly ignore speed limits or willfully cheat on their tax returns. These actions exemplify a desire deep within to do what we want to do, regardless of what others think and regardless of how our actions affect the lives of others. The desire for freedom has been one of the driving forces of human history.

If freedom is the ultimate gift of God to those who put their faith in Christ and if freedom is one of the driving forces of human history, why then is the idea of unlimited freedom a myth? Let me cite two reasons.

For one thing, when we believe we have unlimited freedom, *we misunderstand what freedom is.* We picture freedom as the absence of external constraint, but that is not an accurate picture. Real freedom is not the freedom *from* control but the freedom *of* control. In the words of Charles Kingsley (1819–1875), "There are two freedoms: the false where a man is free to do what he likes; the true where a man is free to do what he ought."[1] Real freedom is not the freedom to do what we want to do. Real freedom is the ability to do what we ought to do. Consequently, our freedom as Christians is always limited by responsibility to be what God calls us and redeems us to be.

In addition, when we believe we have unlimited freedom, *we misunderstand how freedom is experienced.* Like the younger son in Jesus' parable of the prodigal son (Luke 15), we believe that if we can just break away from all the controls on our lives, then we will be free. But that is not how we experience freedom. Real freedom comes not by removing all controls but by submitting ourselves to certain controls. For example, the freedom to excel on a final exam comes through submitting ourselves to the control of a disciplined period of study. The freedom to win a race comes through submitting ourselves to the control of a rigorous regimen of workouts. The freedom to play a violin solo expertly comes through submitting ourselves to the control of years of dedicated practice. We do not experience real freedom by throwing off all restraints. Real freedom comes when we set our eyes on a goal and then impose the necessary restraints to reach that goal. Consequently, our freedom as Christians is limited by the requirements to reach the goal God places before us. True freedom, then, is limited by our responsibility to God and by the purpose to which God calls us.

Apparently the Corinthian Christians also succumb to the myth of unlimited freedom, so Paul addresses the problem in our text. Remember the setting. Paul introduces the key issue confronting the Christians in Corinth in the first part of chapter 8. Should they eat meat that they buy in the marketplace or the meat served at the community banquets since the meat might have been offered previously as a sacrifice to a pagan God? Some of the Christians think food offered to idols is tainted and that to eat it is a sacrilege. Others know that idols do not represent any deity and therefore eating the meat used to worship such nonentities does not affect them at all. If they offend the other uninformed Christians by their actions, so be it.

Against that backdrop, Paul writes these instructions:

> Be careful, however, that the exercise of your freedom does not become a stumbling block to the weak. For if anyone with a weak conscience sees you who have this knowledge eating in an idol's temple, won't he be emboldened to eat what has been sacrificed to idols? So this weak brother, for whom Christ died, is destroyed by your knowledge. When you sin against your brothers in this way and wound their weak conscience, you sin against Christ. Therefore, if what I eat causes my brother to fall into sin, I will never eat meat again, so that I will not cause him to fall. (vv. 9-13)

There is no such thing as unlimited freedom, Paul tells the Corinthians. Instead, our freedom as Christian is limited in two ways.

First, our freedom as Christians is limited *by our relationships with others*. Paul warns in verse 9, *Be careful that the exercise of your freedom does not become a stumbling block to the weak*. We are free in Christ, but our freedom ends at the point where someone else's rights begin. We are not free to do something that will harm another person. We are not free to do something that will lead another Christian astray. There is no such thing as unlimited freedom. Instead, our freedom is limited by our relationships with others.

In addition, our freedom as Christians is limited *by our commitment to Christ. When you sin against your brothers in this way and wound their weak conscience*, Paul tells the Corinthians in verse 12, *you sin against Christ.* We are free in Christ, but our freedom ends at the point where our responsibility to Christ begins. We are not free to do something that will dishonor Christ. We are not free to do something that will hurt the cause of Christ. There is no such thing as unlimited freedom. Instead, our freedom is limited by our relationship with Christ.

We see an extraordinary illustration of true Christian freedom in the life of Dietrich Bonhoeffer, German Christian, leader of the Confessing church that opposed the Nazi regime, and who was eventually executed in a German prison camp in 1945, just days before World War II was over. One biographer identifies three times when Bonhoeffer could have extricated himself from the situation that led ultimately to his death. The first occasion was in 1933, when he went to serve as pastor of a parish in London but decided that his presence was needed with his theological students in Germany. The second was in 1939 when, after having been removed safely to America, he decided to go back to Germany to share the anguish with his people there. The third was the opportunity to escape from prison with the connivance of his guards. He refused to escape because his action would have endangered his brother and uncle who were also in prison. He refused at each point to extricate himself from the situation, his biographer explains, because he was afraid he would compromise his commitment to Christ and endanger those who were left behind. Here was a man with a strong desire to escape and who on three occasions had the opportunity to escape, but he deliberately chose not to because he understood the limitations of his freedom.[2]

Bonhoeffer can instruct us about the true meaning of freedom. If we turn from our responsibility to care for those around us and just do what we want to do, then we are not free. Instead, we lose our freedom, for we have become imprisoned by our own selfish desires. If we turn from our relationship with Christ and do just what we want to do, then we are not free. Instead, we lose our freedom, for we have become imprisoned by our own sinful passions. Freedom is the birthright of every Christian, but freedom must be rightly understood. As Christians, we are free to behave as a Christian in relationship to others, and we are free to do what pleases Christ. We have no freedom beyond that. And that freedom is enough.

Notes

1. Charles L. Wallis, ed., *The Ministers Manual*, 1978 ed. (San Francisco: Harper & Row, 1978) 10.

2. Malcolm Muggeridge, *A Third Testament* (Boston: Little, Brown and Company, 1976) 192.

22

The Church Is Not about Meeting My Needs

1 Corinthians 9:1-27

There is a long-running story (of unknown origin) that in a small town in Tennessee, a sign in front of one of the churches reads, "Left Foot Baptist Church." What a strange name for a church! Originally, a church in that small town practiced foot washing as an ordinance. However, a conflict arose over which foot should be washed first. The group insisting on the left foot taking precedence finally withdrew and split off to organize its own church, and they named their church the Left Foot Baptist Church.[1] If the story is true, somewhere along the way those people lost sight of what it means to be the church.

In more subtle ways, many of us Christians do the same thing. For example, one church surveyed its members. One of the questions was, "What do you expect when you come to worship on Sunday morning?" The most popular answer was, "We expect to be through by 12:00 so we can beat the other churches to the cafeteria." In an exit interview with former church members, another church asked, "Why did you leave our church?" The most common answer was, "We were not being fed." Church growth consultant Win Arn conducted a survey in which he interviewed the members of nearly one thousand churches in regard to what they perceived to be the mission of the church. Eighty-nine percent said the church exists "to take care of my family's and my needs."[2]

We do not have to go to the Left Foot Baptist Church in a small town in Tennessee to discover Christians who have lost sight of what it means to be the church. All we have to do is go to any church in any city and then compare what we hear from church members with what we hear from Jesus in Matthew 16:17-19, and we will discover that somewhere along the way a lot of us have lost sight of what it means to be the church.

In the single most important statement about the church in the Gospels—in Matthew 16:17-19—Jesus does not say anything about meeting our needs or satisfying our spiritual hunger or keeping us happy. Instead, Jesus calls us to abandon our needs and set aside our agenda so that we can participate in God's agenda of bringing the world back into a relationship with him through Jesus Christ. In that pivotal passage, Jesus declares, "On this rock I will build *my* church" (author's italics). Then he explains, "I will give you the keys of the kingdom of heaven; whatever you bind on earth will be bound in heaven, and whatever you lose on earth will be loosed in heaven." Finally, he assures his disciples that when they go out with the keys of the kingdom to fulfill his agenda, "the gates of Hades will not overcome it."

The church is not about meeting our needs or following our agenda. The church is about serving God and fulfilling his kingdom agenda.

Paul faces the same issue with the members of the Corinthian church. Apparently, some of the Corinthian Christians put their own desires and their own needs before the responsibilities of the church and accuse Paul of doing the same thing. Paul answers them in our text with a couple of questions and then an explanation.

In verse 1 Paul asks, *Am I not free?* (The anticipated answer is "Yes.") Freedom is one of the benefits of the Christian life. Jesus sets us free from the control of sin and from the fear of death. Paul recognizes the freedom that is ours in Christ Jesus.

In verse 4 Paul asks, *Don't we have the right to food and drink?* (Again the expected answer is "Yes.") Certain privileges are ours when we serve the Lord. Paul recognizes those privileges. In this passage, he probably has in mind the financial support that should be given to those who lead in the service of the kingdom, and he explains, from Scripture and from common sense, why the worker should be paid for his work. But Paul also recognizes other privileges that come to the Christian. "Am I not free?" Paul asks. "Don't we have the right to food or drink?" Paul asks. The answer to both questions is, "Yes." But then notice how Paul concludes: *But we do not use this right. On the contrary, we put up with anything rather than hinder the gospel of Christ* (v. 12).

Here is Paul's point. Even though certain rights and privileges accompany the Christian life as the natural consequence of our relationship with Christ, the church is not primarily about facilitating these personal privileges. Therefore, whenever we let our concern about our rights and privileges and freedom hinder the spread of the gospel of Christ, then we lose sight of the purpose of the church.

If our focus in the church should not be our rights and our privileges, then where should we focus our energy and effort? Paul provides three answers to that question in the remainder of the chapter.

Instead of focusing on our rights and privileges, we need to focus *on fulfilling our calling* (vv. 16-18). Paul writes, *Yet when I preach the gospel, I cannot boast, for I am compelled to preach. Woe to me if I do not preach the gospel* (v. 16). Paul does not preach because it brings a reward to him. Paul preaches because that is his calling.

When I was seventeen years old, in the spring of my senior year in high school, God called me to the preaching ministry. That was one of the most distinct experiences of my early years, and it has been the driving force in my adult life. God does not call only preachers. God has a calling for every Christian. Paul reminds the Corinthians in a later chapter in this epistle, "There are different kinds of gifts, but the same Spirit. There are different kinds of service, but the same Lord. There are different kinds of working, but the same God works all of them in all men" (12:4-6). Every Christian has a gift, and every Christian has a calling, and the purpose of the church is to help us fulfill our calling.

Consequently, the thoughts that should reverberate through churches are not, "Why are my needs not being met?" or "Why are my opinions not being followed?" Instead, reverberating through our churches should be the sound of people passionately acknowledging the compulsion of their calling, saying "woe to me if I don't work with preschoolers," "woe to me if I don't teach a Sunday school class," "woe to me if I don't lead a prayer group," or "woe to me if I don't sing in the choir."

"I am not worried about my rights," Paul asserts. "I am not concerned with my privileges. I am passionately committed to doing the thing God has called me to do. Woe to me if I do not preach the gospel." That is where we should place our focus in the church.

Instead of focusing on our rights and privileges, we also need to focus on *reaching the world for Christ* (vv. 19-23). Paul writes,

> I make myself a slave to everyone, to win as many as possible. To the Jews I become like a Jew, to win the Jews. To those under the law I became like one under the law, . . . so as to win those under the law. To those not having the law I become like one not having the law, . . . so as to win those not having the law. To the weak I became weak, to win the weak.

> I have become all things to all men so that by all possible means I might save some. (vv. 19-22)

Paul is not concerned about his rights or privileges. One passion burns in his heart, and that passion is to reach the world for Christ. Every instruction of Jesus to the church—when he says "I will give you the keys of the kingdom" (Matt 16:19), "Therefore go and make disciples of all peoples" (Matt 28:19-20), "As the Father has sent me, I am sending you" (John 20:21), and "You will be my witnesses . . . to the ends of the earth" (Acts 1:8)—challenges us to reach out to the world instead of just huddling with our friends inside the church walls.

Paul recognizes that truth and communicates it to the Corinthian Christians. "I am not worried about my rights," Paul affirms. "I am not concerned with my privileges. I am passionately committed to reaching the world for Christ. I have become all things to all people so that, by all possible means, I might save some." That is where we should place our focus in the church.

Finally, instead of focusing on our rights and privileges, we need to focus on *staying engaged in God's work* (vv. 24-27). Paul writes, *Therefore I do not run like a man running aimlessly; I do not fight like a man beating the air. No, I beat my body and make it my slave so that after I have preached to others, I myself will not be disqualified for the prize* (v. 26). Paul gives no thought to what is coming to him and takes no satisfaction in what he has already done. He just wants to make sure that as long as he has life in his body, he will continue to be spiritually fit to do kingdom work. He wants to run the race all the way to the finish line.

In the 1968 Olympics in Mexico City, Mamo Wolde of Ethiopia crossed the finish line to win the Olympic marathon. For more than an hour after he broke the tape, the die-hard spectators watched the other runners come into the Olympic stadium and cross the finish line. Finally, when it looked like all the runners were finished, the remaining spectators who were emptying out of the stadium were interrupted by the sounds of sirens and police whistles coming from the marathon gate into the stadium. One last runner—John Stephen Akhwari from Tanzania—made his way onto the track for the last lap. As he crossed the finish line, the remaining spectators cheered their approval. A reporter asked him why he had not quit since he had no chance of winning a medal. John Stephen Akhwari responded, "My country did not send me to Mexico City to start the race. They sent me to finish the race."[3]

The desire to finish the race drives Paul. "I am not worried about my rights," Paul says. "I am not concerned with my privileges. I just want to be in the middle of what God is doing as long as I have breath in my body. I beat my body and make it my slave so that after I have preached to others, I myself will not be disqualified for the prize." That is where we should place our focus in the church.

The church is not about meeting our needs. The church is not about following our agenda. The purpose of the church is to enable us to fulfill our calling, to equip us to share our witness, and to energize us to do kingdom work.

Notes

1. Michael Hodgin, *1001 More Humorous Illustrations* (Grand Rapids MI: Zondervan Publishing House, 1998) 108.

2. James Emery White, *Rethinking the Church* (Grand Rapids MI: Baker Books, 1997) 30.

3. John C. Maxwell, *Your Road Map for Success* (Nashville: Thomas Nelson Publishers, 2002) 156.

23

Learning from History

1 Corinthians 10:1-11

Comic strip characters Andy Capp and his long-suffering wife Flo are having a conversation. Andy Capp is in a particularly bad mood, deeply depressed. So he says to Flo, "You know, Pet, I ain't worth nothing. That's the truth." His wife responds, hoping to cheer him up. "Don't be so hard on yourself," she tells him. "If nothing else, you serve as a horrible example." With that word of encouragement, Andy Capp heads to the pub with a new bounce in his step, saying to himself, "You know, it's nice to know you're making a contribution."

The Bible often encourages us to learn from the good examples of the past. For example, after a listing of the great heroes of the faith in Hebrews 11, the writer concludes, "Remember your leaders, who spoke the word of God to you. Consider the outcome of their way of life and imitate their faith" (Heb 13:7). Remember the positive examples from the past. Learn from them. Emulate them. That is a common note in Scripture. However, in our text for this chapter Paul challenges his contemporaries in Corinth to remember the negative examples of the past so that they can learn from them as well. Paul believes these horrible examples can also make a contribution to the lives of the Corinthian Christians.

Sometimes we suffer from a kind of amnesia that compels us to overlook negative examples and consequently repeat the same mistakes. That problem also appears among the Corinthian Christians. Their careless amnesia blocks out of their minds some important lessons they should learn from the horrible examples of their history. Paul focuses on these examples in the opening verses of 1 Corinthians 10. Let me set the context for the passage.

Some of the Christians in Corinth have become overconfident in their new status as Christians. They embrace their freedom in Christ. They bask in their rights as believers. They cash in on their privileges as Christians, and they believe that their privileges preclude them from the possibility of falling into sin.

Paul responds to them by saying, "If you think you are so privileged, remember the Israelites. They had all kinds of special privileges." He asserts, that their ancestors *were all under the cloud* (v. 1). The cloud represents the Shekinah presence of God (Exod 16:10, 1 Kings 8:10, 2 Chr 5:13). These Israelites, Paul explains, experienced the very presence of God visibly before them. He adds, "they all passed through the sea" (10:1). The parting of the sea as the Israelites escaped from Egypt symbolizes God's guidance in their lives. So these Israelites not only experienced God's presence but also received God's personal guidance in their lives. Paul continues by reminding the Corinthians that the Hebrews *all ate the same spiritual food* (v. 3) and *drank the same spiritual drink* (v. 4). Paul alludes to the manna God provided from heaven and the water God provided from the rock when Moses struck it with his staff. Paul calls both the food and water spiritual because of the supernatural way in which God provided these things. God gave these Israelites his supernatural provisions.

Do you get the picture? These Israelites had everything going for them. They experienced the presence of God. They observed the power of God. They received the provisions of God. Yet, Paul concludes that even they fell into sin and as a result, *their bodies were scattered over the desert* (v. 5). Or, as the New American Standard Bible puts it, *They were laid low in the wilderness* (v. 5). The Israelites thought they had it made. They thought they were invulnerable, but then temptation came and laid them low.

With this background, Paul reminds the Corinthian Christians, *Now these things occurred as examples to keep us from setting our hearts on evil things as they did* (v. 6). The Corinthian Christians need to learn from these horrible examples in their history. What do the Corinthians need to learn from these horrible examples? Paul explains beginning in verse 7.

In verse 7, Paul writes, *Do not be idolaters, as some of them were; as it is written: 'The people sat down to eat and drink and got up to indulge in pagan revelry.'* Paul refers here to the experience of the Hebrews waiting for Moses to come down from Mt. Sinai, recorded in Exodus 32. After persuading Aaron to construct a golden calf for them to worship, the Israelites ate a sacrificial meal in dedication to the calf and then got up to dance in ceremonial revelry (Exod 32:6), just as the pagans danced before their gods.

Why was this action a sin? When God made covenant with Israel, he called them to an exclusive commitment to him. "I am the Lord your God, who brought you out of Egypt, out of the land of slavery," God reminded

Israel. And then he added, "You shall have no other gods before me" (Exod 20:2-3). Yet, instead of being faithful to the covenant God, these Israelites quickly gave their allegiance to more manageable and more comfortable gods. They turned to idolatry, and as a result, *They were laid low in the wilderness* (v. 5, NASB).

In verses 8, Paul writes, "We should not commit sexual immorality, as some of them did—and in one day twenty-three thousand of them died." Paul refers here to the incident described in Numbers 25:1-9 when Israel joined with the Moabites in the worship of Baal of Peor. The Moabites worshiped their god through the prostitution of virgins. In other words, idolatry and sexual immorality became intermeshed.

Why was this action a sin? When God made covenant with Israel, he placed certain requirements on them. We call that list of requirements the Ten Commandments. At the heart of the Ten Commandments stands this unequivocal demand: "You shall not commit adultery" (Exod 20:14). God called his people to be a holy people, but instead of remaining sexually pure, they participated in the sexual orgies of their pagan neighbors. They lapsed into immorality, and as a result, *They were laid low in the wilderness* (v. 5, NASB).

In verse 9, Paul writes, "We should not test the Lord, as some of them did—and were killed by snakes." Paul refers here to the event described in Numbers 21 when the Hebrews began to complain about how God was taking care of them. "There is no food," they whined, "and no water, and we loathe this miserable manna" (Num 21:5). In other words, they complained that their needs were not being met. Suddenly fiery serpents surrounded them and thousands of Hebrews were killed until, finally, following the command of God, Moses lifted up a serpent on a pole, and those who looked to the serpent were spared.

Why was this action a sin? When God made covenant with Israel, he gave them a mission to be the channels of his blessing to the world. However, instead of focusing on God and his mission, they focused on themselves and their needs. They turned their attention inward, and as a result, *They were laid low in the wilderness* (v. 5, NASB).

In verse 10, Paul writes, "And do not grumble, as some of them did—and were killed by the destroying angel." Paul refers here to the event at Kadesh Barnea, recorded in Numbers 14, when the people complained about Moses' leadership, whining that they would have rather died in Egypt. As a result, God sent a "destroying angel" to bring the plague spoken of in Numbers 14:37. Paul alludes to their critical spirit, to what we might call grumbling or fault finding. I heard one preacher refer to this as "leadership from the rear"—individuals who are not willing to lead out in God's kingdom work but who, from the rear, criticize those who are leading.

Why was this action a sin? When God made covenant with Israel he called Moses to be the leader for the people of God, to lead them out of Egypt, and to lead them into the promised land. But instead of following Moses' leadership, the Israelites grumbled and complained and criticized, and as a result, *They were laid low in the wilderness* (v. 5, NASB).

Paul does not randomly select these four examples from Hebrew history. On the contrary, he chooses these four specific examples because in a precise way they reflect the situation in Corinth. The Corinthian Christians also turn to other gods besides the God who revealed himself in Jesus Christ and called them to do kingdom work in Corinth. The Corinthian Christians also wink at immorality in their lives and follow the permissive lifestyle of the Corinthian culture instead of the disciplined lifestyle of the Christian life. The Corinthian Christians also focus on their rights and privileges instead of fulfilling their calling to engage in kingdom work. The Corinthian Christians also grumble about Paul's leadership and hold back the work of God in the church instead of giving themselves to the kingdom work God called them to do. Paul presents to the Corinthian Christians these four horrible examples from their past and announces, *Now these things occurred as examples to keep us from setting our hearts on evil things as they did* (v. 6).

These examples reflect behavior that often appears in today's church. Consequently, Paul's warning comes to us as well. When we give our allegiance to any god other than the missionary God who calls us to a missionary task, when we allow the immorality that is around us to move within us, when we focus all our attention on our rights and our privileges and what we have coming to us, or when we spend all our time grumbling about how things are done and who is in charge, then we too will miss the opportunity God gives us to be significant players in his kingdom work. Someday someone will look back at us and say, *They had such an opportunity. They were poised for greatness. But they repeated the mistakes of their ancestors, they failed to learn from history, and as a result, 'They were laid low in the wilderness'* (v. 5, NASB).

24

Two Inescapable Truths about the Christian Life

1 Corinthians 10:12–13

Someone once asked well-known American historian Charles A. Beard what lessons he learned in his lifelong study of history. He said he learned four lessons: the bee fertilizes the flower from which it steals, those whom the gods would destroy they first make mad, when it gets dark enough you can see the stars, and the wheels of God grind slowly but they grind exceedingly fine.[1]

Snoopy, a well-known comic strip character, learned another lesson about life. Standing on his doghouse, he cowers before Lucy who is climbing up onto his doghouse, snarling, "I've taken enough of your insults, you stupid dog!" She continues, "I'm gonna pound you! I'm gonna fix you good." Snoopy looks around for a way to escape. She shouts, "Don't look around. There's no way out! No way!" Snoopy leans backward with Lucy in his face as she tells him, "You've had it, dog. Prepare to meet your doom!" At about that time, Snoopy leans forward and kisses Lucy right on the lips! Lucy turns in disgust, muttering, "Augh!" as she falls off the other side of the doghouse. In the final frame, Snoopy rests peacefully on the top of his doghouse and pronounces the basic truth he discovered about life. He says, "One kiss is worth two judo chops anytime!"

Country singer Randy Travis encompasses his philosophy of life in a song titled "Don't Ever Sell Your Saddle." It goes like this:

> Trouble always starts as fun,
> And broken hearts will always mend.
> Tough times don't last, tough people do,
> And nothing breaks if it can bend.
> Don't ever sell your saddle,

Never owe another man.
Watch where you spit on a windy day
Don't use words you don't understand.
Find the Lord before you need him.
And never lose your pride.
Don't ever sell your saddle.
For life's a long, long ride.[2]

A famous historian, a comic strip character, and a country singer give their insights into the basic truths about life. Their comments certainly deserve our consideration. We should give even more consideration to the words of the Apostle Paul who, under the inspiration of the Holy Spirit, communicates to the ages about the true meaning of life.

In this letter known as 1 Corinthians, Paul instructs the Christians in Corinth on how to contextualize the gospel in the midst of a pagan culture. Multiple issues confront them as they fulfill this challenge, and Paul addresses these issues in his epistle. The immorality of the culture keeps seeping into the church. Paul addresses that issue in chapter 5. Conflicts arise among the Christians as egos get in the way. Paul addresses that issue in chapter 6. They have questions about marriage. Should they even get married, and if they do, how does their Christian faith affect their relationship as husbands and wives? Paul addresses that issue in chapter 7. The issue of their freedom as Christians and how they are to express that freedom absorbs Paul's attention in chapters 8 and 9. Then, in chapter 10, Paul reminds the Corinthians of the lessons they need to learn from the horrible examples in their history—the dangers of idolatry and immorality and mixed priorities and grumbling. In the midst of these specific suggestions for specific problems, it seems as if Paul steps back in 10:12-13 to take the broad view by presenting two inescapable truths about the Christian life.

The first inescapable truth, presented in verse 12, can be simply stated: *anybody can fall.* Paul warns, *So, if you think you are standing firm, be careful that you don't fall!* I will illustrate Paul's warning with a biblical story about Solomon, the son of David, the third king of the United Kingdom of Israel.

The biblical writer acknowledges Solomon's remarkable beginning in 1 Kings 3. To show his gratitude to God, Solomon goes to Gibeon and offers a sacrifice to God—a thousand burnt offerings (3:4). In response to his offering, God appears to Solomon in a dream and tells him, "Ask for whatever you want me to give you" (3:5). Can you imagine such an offer? The creator God who holds the whole world in his hands, the sovereign God who owns the cattle on a thousand hills, the God who can do exceedingly more than all we ask or even think tells Solomon, "Ask for whatever you want me to give you."

How will Solomon respond? Solomon says, "Now, O Lord my God, you have made your servant king in place of my father David. But I am only a little child and do not know how to carry out my duties. . . . So give your servant a discerning heart to govern your people and to distinguish between right and wrong" (3:7, 9). God responds, "Great answer, Solomon. Because you asked for wisdom, I will give you wisdom. But I will also give you all the other things you did not ask for—power, wealth, and fame" (3:10-13, author's paraphrase).

What a beginning for Solomon. With that beginning, with that attitude, and with those blessings, surely Solomon will stay strong in his relationship with God all the days of his life. Yet he does not. At the end of his reign, the biblical writer says about Solomon, "As Solomon grew old, his wives turned his heart after other gods, and his heart was not fully devoted to the Lord his God, as the heart of David his father had been" (1 Kings 11:4).

Here is the lesson articulated by Paul and illustrated by Solomon: a good beginning does not ensure a good ending. A heart for the Lord at one point in our lives does not guarantee a heart for the Lord at every point in our lives. God anoints Solomon as his king and makes him perhaps the wisest man who ever lived, yet his heart turns after other gods. If he can fall, so can any one of us.

So, if you think you are standing firm, Paul warns, *be careful that you don't fall!* Anybody can fall—that is the first inescapable truth about life in our text.

We see the second inescapable truth in verse 13: *anybody can stand.* Paul explains, *No temptation has seized you except what is common to man. And God is faithful; he will not let you be tempted beyond what you can bear. But when you are tempted, he will also provide a way out so that you can stand up under it.* I will illustrate Paul's promise with a biblical story about Joseph, the favorite son of Jacob, the privileged son with the coat of many colors.

The biblical writer tells an amazing story about Joseph in Genesis 39. At this point Joseph has already been sold into slavery by his brothers, but as a slave he demonstrates a remarkable ability. God seems to bless him in a particular way. So Potiphar, the captain of Pharaoh's guard, puts Joseph in charge of his household, the Bible says, and "entrusted to his care everything he owned" (39:4). Then the biblical writer tells us something that sounds like a script for one of our modern-day soap operas: "Now Joseph was well-built and handsome, and after a while his master's wife took notice of Joseph and said, 'Come to bed with me!'" (39:6-7). Joseph refuses.

But the story does not end here. Day after day, Potiphar's wife continues to seduce Joseph. Day after day she invites him into her bed. He is just a Hebrew slave. She is the mistress of the house. What can he do? He can say, "No." He can resist, and he does. Then one day she catches him at a moment when all the other servants are gone. She grabs him by his cloak and demands, "Right now, I want you to come to bed with me." The Bible says, "He left his cloak in her hand and ran out of the house" (39:12). Joseph said, "No."

Joseph is just a slave. He has no power. He is at the mercy of the mistress of the house. Yet he refuses to yield to temptation but instead looks for the way out so that he will be able to escape. If he can stand, so can any of us.

No temptation has seized you except what is common to man, Paul explains. *And God is faithful; he will not let you be tempted beyond what you can bear. But when you are tempted, he will also provide a way out so that you can stand up under it* (vv. 12-13). That is the second inescapable truth about the Christian life in our text.

One of Harry Truman's biographers captures the essence of the former president's success in a single sentence. The biographer says, "An almost equal resistance to both euphoria and despair was one of his most considerable qualities."[3] Paul calls for that kind of balance in our text, an almost equal resistance to the euphoria of overconfidence on the one hand and the despair of resignation on the other hand. Anyone can fall, so don't gloat. And anyone can stand, so don't despair. These are two inescapable truths about the Christian life.

Notes

1. Stephen Brown, *If God Is in Charge* (Nashville: Thomas Nelson Publishers, 1983) 163.

2. Randy Travis, "Don't Ever Sell Your Saddle," *Inspirational Journey*, Warner/ Reprise/ Maverick, 2000.

3. Roy Jenkins, *Truman* (New York: Harper & Row, 1986) 42.

25

Choosing Sides

1 Corinthians 10:14-22

The Karankawa inhabited the lower gulf plains of southern Texas and northern Mexico. The coming of the Anglos to their area, along with new diseases against which they had no immunity and the killing of the buffalo, decimated the tribe. Their final demise came during the Texas Revolution. Captain Dimmit, a Texan, gave the members of the tribe some beef from his ranch whenever they came by. With the start of the war, however, the captain left to serve with the Texas army. The Karankawa knew nothing about this war. They went by Captain Dimmit's ranch and, not seeing him there, they rounded up a few cattle as they always had. A party of Mexican soldiers approached and asked what they were doing. When they said they were friends of Captain Dimmit, the Mexicans attacked, killing many of them and causing the others to flee. Soon they met another party of soldiers who happened to be Texans. Those who remained from the tribe wanted to avoid another assault, so they cried out, "Viva, Mexico!" At that point, the Texas army attacked them and killed off most of the rest of the tribe.[1]

Paul fears the Corinthian Christians will suffer at the hands of fellow believers if they don't identify themselves clearly as Christians, so he returns to the earlier debate about eating food in one of the fellowship meals in someone's home that might have been offered as a sacrifice to idols. This issue created by the meat offered to idols presents the new believers in Corinth with a pressing dilemma. Idols not only dominate the spiritual life of Corinth but also the social life of the people. These meals are the "in" thing in the city of Corinth. The guests at these banquets make the headlines of the current issue of *C Magazine*, and many of the believers in Corinth have participated in these meals before becoming Christians. Now that they are Christians, they wonder if they should continue to participate in these feasts to the pagan gods and thereby identify with the idols of their culture.

Some of the new believers in Corinth believe they can participate in these feasts without compromising their faith. Two convictions motivate them. For one thing, since idols are not real but are only figments of someone's imagination, eating the food offered to idols and even participating in the meals with those who worship these idols does not mean anything. Therefore, they feel free to participate in these meals just as they did before. In addition, as long as they participate in the sacred meal offered at church, that is, as long as they are church members in good standing, they believe they will be protected from falling under the influence of these pagan idols and those who worship them. They explain to Paul their justification for participating in these feats and request his opinion on the matter.

Before we hear Paul's response to them, let us try to connect with the situation in our text. Paul's words in our text are not simply meant to be a history lesson informing us about the issues facing Christians in the first-century city of Corinth. Instead, Paul's words should also instruct us about issues facing us as Christians in the twenty-first century. Clearly, people around us today still worship idols, but not necessarily the kinds of idols they construct out of wood or position on a table in their family rooms. Pleasure and comfort and money and popularity and power—those are the preferred idols of our day. The worship of these idols dominates life in America. The question facing us is this: as Christians, how are we to relate to these idols of our day?

In answering that question, some twenty-first-century Christians use the same arguments the Corinthian Christians use. They might say, "These idols of our pagan culture—pleasure, comfort, money, popularity, power—are not real, and therefore they have no power over our lives. Consequently, it does not hurt us to be involved with them." Or they might say, "As long as we go to church on Sunday, it really does not matter what we do during the week. We are safe." Many Christians today do the same things and use the same justifications the Corinthian Christians of the first century employ.

How does Paul respond to Christians today who seem unconcerned about the worship of idols and to his contemporaries in Corinth who continue to attend these feasts? Paul says, "Nonsense! You cannot have it both ways. You cannot be a member in good standing with the Christian community on the one hand and blend in comfortably with the pagan community on the other hand. These are mutually exclusive groups. You have to choose sides." That is Paul's message in our text. Let us unpack Paul's argument and then apply his word to our lives today.

Paul begins with a clear command that the Corinthian Christians cannot possibly misunderstand: *Therefore, my dear friends, flee from idolatry* (v. 14). Paul's prohibition is both absolute and unmistakable. It echoes the earlier statement by Jesus himself. In Matthew 6:24, Jesus declares, "No one can serve two masters. Either he will hate the one and love the other, or he will be devoted to the one and despise the other. You cannot serve both God and Money." By "money," Jesus refers to the value system of the world. In other words, a person cannot live by the value system of the kingdom of God and the value system of the world at the same time. These are two mutually exclusive lifestyles. We have to choose. We will either choose to worship God and organize our lives around him, or we will worship some idol—pleasure or comfort or money or popularity or power—and organize our lives around it.

After presenting this principle, Paul supports it by appealing to the people's common sense (v. 15). "Use your head," he says to the Corinthian believers. "Think about what it means to participate in the church." He uses the observance of the Lord's Supper as an illustration. Something inherent in the nature of the Christian meal we know as the Lord's Supper makes participation in the pagan meals of the world incompatible, and that something is *koinonia*, a word that in its deepest meaning carries the idea of participation. When we take the cup, we participate with the Lord. When we share the bread, we participate with each other (vv. 16-17). These unique relationships with Christ and with other Christians make it impossible for us to be associated in the same way with the pagans.

Paul further illustrates his point with a reference to the offering of sacrifices by the Israelites (v. 18). Again his point seems to be that participating in the sacrifices to God implies a connection with or commitment to God that makes any connection with idols incompatible.

Paul then takes his argument a step further. Some of the Corinthian Christians claim that since the idols are not real, eating the meat that has been offered to them is harmless, as is participating in the feasts with those who worship these idols. Paul warns them not to underestimate the malevolent effect of these idols. He reminds them that *the sacrifices of pagans are offered to demons, not to God, and I do not want you to be participants with demons* (v. 20).

We can summarize Paul's response to the Corinthian Christians with two conclusions. First, participating in the fellowship of the church does not give the Corinthian Christians license to do whatever they want to do. Rather, their participation in the fellowship of the church binds them to one another and to Christ in such a way that they are only free to do what honors Christ and builds up other believers. Second, participating in fellowship with those in the world is not a harmless activity. Instead, it is an activity fraught with danger, for the idols of the world are part of the system of evil that stands over against God (Eph 6:12). To align with them is to align against the kingdom of God.

Now let us apply these two conclusions to our lives today.

On the one hand, Paul wants us to understand that *participating in the fellowship of the church is a demanding choice.* The church is not a country club where we simply hang out with others like us. The church is not a hospital that we turn to only when we have needs to be met. Instead, the church is a *koinonia.* Paul uses that word three times in our text to describe the church (10:16; 10:18; 10:20). This word does not just mean that we like to spend time with each other as believers. This word suggests that we are inextricably connected with each other in a sacred task that demands the best effort we can offer.

A little boy goes to school for his first day as a first grader. At lunchtime he packs up his crayons, papers, scissors, and paste and heads out the door. His teacher asks, "Tommy, where are you going? It's time for lunch." Tommy, used to his half-day of kindergarten, replies, "I always go home when the other kids go to eat. I'll come back tomorrow." "No, Tommy," the teacher explains. "That was last year when you were in kindergarten. This year you stay all day. You go to lunch and then you come back in the afternoon to study and do more work. You are only halfway through for the day. You have a lot more to do before you go home." Tommy thinks about this for a moment. Then he shakes his head in frustration. Turning to his teacher, he protests, "Who signed me up for that?"

Some Christians might feel that way about the church. They want the church to meet their needs. They want the church to teach the Bible to their children. They want the church to be there for them on the special occasions of their lives, but when they realize that the church is more than that, they cry out in frustration, "Who signed me up for that?" The answer is, "We did." When we sign up for Christ, we commit ourselves to participate in kingdom work. We are no longer free to set our own agendas. We are no longer free to do what we want to do. We are no longer to be focused just on our needs. We have committed ourselves to give priority to and organize our lives around God's kingdom work. Participating in the fellowship of the church is a demanding choice.

In addition, Paul wants us to understand that *participating in the fellowship of the church is a dangerous choice.* The value system of the world is not neutral. The idols of the world are not powerless. Instead, the world is an aggressive, intimidating force that stands against the kingdom of God (v. 20). The forces of the world will line up against us when we make the choice to give ourselves completely to kingdom causes.

Jim Elliot paid the ultimate price for his participation in the work of the kingdom. Born in Portland, Oregon, in 1927, Jim embraced the Christian teachings of his parents and became an outspoken believer during his high school days. At Wheaton College, he sensed God's leadership in his life in the area of missions. During a training camp for missionaries, he learned about the Waodani people, also known as Auca Indians, an indigenous tribe in Ecuador who were considered violent and dangerous to outsiders. In 1952, he and a friend, Peter Fleming, traveled to Ecuador to evangelize the Auca Indians. He was soon joined by others, along with Elisabeth Howard, whom he married in 1953. They made some contact with the Auca Indians using a loudspeaker and a basket to pass down gifts. After several months, they built a base a short distance from the Auca village. Friendly encounters with a few of the natives encouraged them to visit the village, but before they could make the visit, a group of the Auca Indians attacked them and killed Elliot and his four companions.[2] Sometimes, like for Jim Elliot and his fellow missionaries, choosing to participate in the fellowship of the church puts us in harm's way.

And yet, as difficult as it is and as dangerous as it is, we nevertheless are confronted by the choice. Both Paul in his message to the Corinthian Christians and Jesus in his pronouncement in the Sermon on the Mount (Matt 6:24) remind us that we cannot participate in the table of the Lord and in the table of idols at the same time. These are mutually exclusive decisions. We have to choose.

Notes

1. Richard Shenkman and Kurt Reiger, *One-Night Stands with American History* (New York: HarperCollins, 2003) 68–69.

2. Elisabeth Elliot, *Through Gates of Splendor* (Carol Stream IL: Tyndale House Publishers, 1956) 191–236.

26

Absolutes and Nonessentials

1 Corinthians 10:23-33

A woman went to a pet store and purchased a parrot to keep her company. She took the parrot home but returned to the store the next day to report, "That parrot hasn't said a word yet!"

"Does it have a mirror?" the storekeeper asked. "Parrots like to be able to look at themselves in the mirror."

The woman bought a mirror and took it home. The next day she was back, announcing that the bird still was not speaking.

"What about a ladder?" the storekeeper said. "Parrots enjoy walking up and down a ladder."

She bought a ladder and took it home. The next day she was back—still no words from the parrot.

"Does the parrot have a swing?" the storekeeper asked. "Birds enjoy relaxing on a swing."

She bought a swing and took it home. The next day she returned to the store to announce that the bird had died.

"I'm terribly sorry," the storekeeper said. "Did the bird ever saying anything before it died?"

"Yes," the lady reported. "Just before he died, he said, 'Don't they sell any birdseed at that store?'"

The parrot died because this woman was unable to distinguish between absolutes and nonessentials. The mirror, the ladder, the swing—those were nonessentials. The birdseed was an absolute.

One of life's most important challenges is to determine which tasks deserve priority and which are less important. Steven Covey, in his book *First Things First,* discusses this challenge by blocking our lives into four quadrants. Quadrant I includes things that are important and urgent, like handling an irate customer or church member. Quadrant II includes things that are important but not urgent like exercising and staying fit. Quadrant III includes things that are not important but urgent like fellow workers who interrupt our schedule. Quadrant IV includes things that are not important or urgent like junk e-mails. Unfortunately, most of us spend most of our time in Quadrant IV, which Covey calls the Quadrant of Waste, in Quadrant III, which Covey calls the Quadrant of Deception, or in Quadrant I, where we are at the mercy of the tyranny of the urgent. We should spend most of our time in Quadrant II, which Covey calls the Quadrant of Quality.[1] He is talking about absolutes and nonessentials—learning to distinguish between them and giving our priority attention to the absolutes.

Years earlier, another popular writer put it like this: "The job is, however, not to set priorities. That is easy. Everybody can do it. The reason why so few executives concentrate is the difficulty of setting 'posteriorities'—that is, deciding what tasks not to tackle—and of sticking to the decision."[2]

Distinguishing between absolutes and nonessentials so that we can give our priority attention to the absolutes is one of the most important challenges of life. The challenge of determining priorities and posteriorities also faces the Christian. Many demands come to us as followers of Jesus Christ. Which are absolutes? Which, on the other hand, are nonessentials?

Paul deals with that problem in his letter to the Corinthian Christians, and even though the setting is different from our situation today, the suggestions given by the Apostle Paul are nevertheless relevant. The Corinthian believers face the challenge of being the church in the context of Corinth, a pagan city full of idolatry and immorality. The particular issue that demands their attention is the food sacrificed to idols, some of which would be sold on the open market and some of which would be the primary item on the menu in the societal feasts to which these new Christians were invited. In 1 Corinthians 10:25-26, Paul recommends that the Corinthian Christians purchase meat from the market and eat it as a gift from God. "It is harmless," Paul assures them. "Don't worry about it." In 1 Corinthians 10:27-30, Paul recommends that the Corinthian Christians should refrain from eating meat in someone else's house if it bothers the conscience of some of the other Christians. In either case, Paul seems to suggest, "Eating the meat is a nonessential. Whether the Corinthian believers eat the meat or do not eat the meat, that choice will not bring them closer to God or drive them further away from God. It is a nonessential."

On the other hand, Paul adds, some things are absolutely essential, and the key challenge of the Christian life, then and now, is to distinguish between the absolutes and the nonessentials. Then we must prioritize the absolutes and posteriorize the non-essentials.

What are the absolutes? Paul identifies them in the final verses of our text, one in verse 31 and the other in verse 33.

In 1 Corinthians 10:31, Paul writes, *So whether you eat or drink or whatever you do, do it all for the glory of God.* That is an absolute according to Paul. That must be given priority. What does it mean to do all things to the glory of God? Perhaps the most helpful answer to that question comes from Webster's dictionary that defines "glorify" as "to make, or make seem, better, larger, or more beautiful."[3] To do all things to the glory of God, then, means to do everything in our lives in such a way that God will look better, larger, and more beautiful to those who observe us. God's reputation in the world is determined by how we relate to others, what we say, and how we conduct our lives.

In one of his sermons, I heard James W. Moore, senior pastor of St. Luke's United Methodist Church in Houston, tell the story of a hectic day in his life when he once again discovered how our actions can influence what others think of God. He had to deal with one emergency after another all day. In the middle of the afternoon, as he drove to another important meeting, he realized he had not eaten. Since he had meetings scheduled until late at night, he decided to stop and get a quick sandwich, even though he only had fifteen minutes. Unfortunately, he happened to get in the line of the slowest sandwich-maker in America. The lady behind the counter picked up a piece of bread and smiled at him. She spread mayonnaise on the bread and set it down. Then she picked up another piece of bread and put mayonnaise on it. Next she picked up a piece of turkey breast and slowly folded it on the bread, and then added another piece. She moved as slow as the proverbial turtle. Finally, his patience ran out and he opened his mouth to tell her, "Just forget the sandwich. I do not have time. I will just have to starve to death, thank you very much!"

But before he could get any words out, she asked, "Aren't you the pastor of the St. Luke's Methodist Church?"

He replied, "Yes, ma'am."

"I can't believe this," she responded with a big smile. "My husband will be thrilled to know you were here. We watch you every Sunday on television. He had a stroke about three years ago, and the highlight of his week is watching you preach on Sunday. You are such a wonderful preacher. You have taught us so much about God. Would you sign this napkin so I can show him you came in? He will be absolutely thrilled!" Then she added, "By the way, were you about to say something?"

The pastor replied, "I was just about to say that you certainly do make a fine sandwich."

What if he had lost his temper? What if he had chewed her out for her slowness? What would she have thought about God or about the church? We get so uptight about our schedules and our desires and the important things we think we have to do, but these are nonessentials. What is absolute is doing everything to the glory of God. God's reputation is determined by how we relate to others, what we say, and how we conduct our lives.

In 1 Corinthians 10:33 Paul writes, *For I am not seeking my own good but the good of many, so that they may be saved.* That is an absolute. That must be given priority. Paul clarifies this absolute by setting two things in contrast: being a stumbling block in verse 32 against being a blessing in verse 33. He writes, *Do not cause anyone to stumble, whether Jews, Greeks, or the church of God—even as I try to please everyone in every way* (vv. 32-33). Paul does not suggest that we go through life as people pleasers, never doing anything to hurt someone else's feelings. He simply refuses to do anything that will cause him to stand between the truth of the gospel and those who need to hear the gospel. Again, sometimes whether or not a person becomes a Christian is determined by how we relate to others, what we say, and how we conduct our lives.

I heard a pastor tell in a sermon about how he discovered this truth. His church sat next to a large university. One Sunday a college student walked to the front to make his profession of faith. Whenever a person acknowledged a profession of faith in Christ in this church, the pastor always called to the front the individual most responsible for that decision. He asked the student, "What person most influenced you to make your decision for Christ?"

The student said to the pastor, "You did."

The answer perplexed the pastor because he did not know this young man or remember having a conversation with him. So he asked, "What do you mean? How did I lead you to Christ?"

The student explained, "I watched how you lived and listened to what you said, and the two matched up."

What if the pastor had lived differently? What if he had not treated people right? What would that student have thought about God or about the church? We get so uptight about our freedoms and our privileges and the desire to do our own thing, but these are nonessentials. What is absolute is doing everything possible to lead other people into a relationship with Christ.

Those are the absolutes in the Christian life, Paul declares: giving glory to God and seeking the good of others. Where does Paul get that idea? He gets it from Jesus. When a lawyer approaches Jesus with the question, "Teacher, which is the greatest commandment in the Law?" (Matt 22:36), Jesus answers, "'Love the Lord your God with all your heart and with all your soul and with all your mind.' This is the first and greatest commandment. And the second is like it: 'Love your neighbor as yourself.' All the Law and the Prophets hang on these two commandments" (Matt 22:37-40). Exalting God and encouraging others are the absolutes in the Christian life. We should prioritize those challenges and posteriorize everything else.

Notes

1. Stephen R. Covey, A. Roger Merrill, and Rebecca R. Merrill, *First Things First* (New York: Simon & Schuster, 1994) 37–38.

2. Peter F. Drucker, *The Effective Executive* (New York: Harper & Row, 1966) 109–10.

3. *Webster's New World Dictionary of the American Language* (Nashville: The Southwestern Company, 1965) 319.

27

The Right Attitude in Worship

1 Corinthians 11:1–16

Ian McEwan wrote one of the best-selling fiction books of 2001. This book, *Atonement*, also became a major motion picture. The story begins on a summer day in 1935 when thirteen-year-old Briony Tallis witnesses from an upstairs room an incident between her older sister, Cecilia, and Robbie Turner, the son of a servant. The incident takes place at a fountain in the front yard. Briony can see them but cannot hear their conversation. As she observes this pantomime played out before her, she completely misunderstands what happens. What actually happens is this: Cecilia takes a priceless family vase full of flowers out to the fountain to fill it with water. When Robbie tries to help, he breaks the vase, and two pieces fall into the fountain. This upsets Cecilia so much that she takes off her blouse and skirt, and with only her underclothes on, she steps into the fountain, holds her nose, and goes down to get the pieces of the vase. When she comes out, she put her clothes back on and angrily runs into the house.

Briony sees something altogether different. From a distance, without the benefit of the dialogue, with her incomplete grasp of the dynamics of the relationship between Cecilia and Robbie, and with her vivid imagination working full speed, this is what Briony thinks happened: She thinks Robbie proposes to Cecilia, and then, when he raises his hand, Cecilia immediately takes off her clothes. What mysterious power, Briony wonders, does Robbie have over her sister? When Cecilia steps into the fountain and submerges herself in the water, Briony wonders if she is attempting to commit suicide. Has Robbie broken her heart? When she comes back out of the water, Briony decides her sister has changed her mind about drowning herself, broken free from the mysterious control Robbie has over her, and regained her senses.

She watches her sister storm off after refusing Robbie's request for marriage. Briony's confusion about what happens and her precocious imagination bring about a crime that will change all of their lives forever. You will have to read the book to discover what that crime is. However, my point is that what happens between Cecilia and Robbie differs considerably from what Briony thinks happened. Because she does not understand the context and does not grasp the dynamics at work, she completely misinterprets the situation.[1]

That often happens when we try to understand the experiences described in the Bible. We interpret the events from our perspective instead of from the perspective of the time in which the events occur. As a result, we fail to grasp the dynamics that are at work in the experiences. Like Briony in Ian McEwan's story, we end up completely misunderstanding the meaning of the experience.

We often make that mistake when trying to interpret our text for this chapter. At our first reading of the text, with our twenty-first-century ears, we may conclude that this is one of those instances in which male chauvinist Paul limits the role of women in the leadership of the church and asserts the superiority of the male species. In other words, we conclude that Paul puts women in their place. Paul does make a reference to women in this text, as he will again in chapter 14. But what does Paul actually say? Let us look more closely at the text.

Notice, in verses 4-5, that Paul does not address only the women. Instead, he addresses both the men and the women. To the men, in verse 4, Paul says, *Every man who prays or prophesies with his head covered dishonors his head.* Why does Paul not want the men to cover their heads? The answer grows out of the context. Those men who lead the public meetings in Corinth wear a veil or a toga over their heads to illustrate their importance. Apparently, the Christian men in Corinth follow the same practice in worship for the same reason. They cover their heads with their togas, following the pattern of the pagan leaders, affirming their superiority over the average, run-of-the-meal worshipers who do not prophesy or lead in prayer. Paul instructs them not to do that. "Quit showing off," he warns them. "Quit following the pattern of the pagans. Your glory is not in you; your glory is in the fact that you have been made for God and belong to God." That is why Paul tells the men, *Every man who prays or prophesies with his head covered dishonors his head* (v. 4).

To the women, in verse 5, Paul says, *And every woman who prays or prophesies with her head uncovered dishonors her head.* Why does Paul want the women to cover their heads? Again, the answer grows out of the context.

In the ancient city of Corinth, the marriage ceremony involves "veiling the bride." Therefore, any married woman who wants to be proper will cover her head when she goes out in public. However, another group of women in the city of Corinth, not the proper wives but women known as the *hetairai*, the female companions of the Roman men, what we might call high-class prostitutes, flaunt their freedom and their pursuit of pleasure by uncovering their heads. Apparently, some of the wives in Corinth choose to rebel against the expectations and take off their veils just like the *hetairai*. Some of the Christian women in Corinth follow the same practice. They take off their veils, for instance, when they go to church and stand up to prophesy and to pray. So Paul instructs them not to do that. "Quit following the pattern of the pagans," he warns them. "If you want to look like a prostitute, just shave your head, and then everyone will know for sure! Your freedom is not the freedom to do what you want; you are only free to do what brings glory to God." That is why Paul tells the women, *And every woman who prays or prophesies with her head uncovered dishonors her head* (v. 5).

For the men to exalt themselves by putting on the veils and for the women to debase themselves by taking off the veils implies that the church merely reflects the values and practices of the community. Paul does not want them to do this. He wants them to reflect kingdom values and the unique practices of the church.

This issue becomes crucial to the Corinthian Christians at two points. On the one hand, how the Christian men and women conduct themselves in their weekly religious gatherings will determine the attitude the citizens of Corinth have toward the church (vv. 7-10). The pagans in Corinth look with suspicion on this new religious group that meets every week. What goes on in these weekly gatherings? Are these Christians involved in something seditious, or are they just weird? Since the vestibules of Roman houses in Corinth are open to the street, outsiders can observe the Christians as they gather in the home for worship. Paul identifies these observers as "messengers" (a better translation here than the word "angels") who will perhaps report on the Christians to the authorities. Consequently, because of the suspicion the pagan Corinthians have about the Christian gatherings, because the Corinthian culture is a male-dominated culture, and because at any time an information-gatherer can be in their midst to report back to the authorities, Paul recommends that the women conduct themselves in worship in a way that is beyond reproach.

On the other hand, how the Christian men and women conduct themselves in their weekly religious gatherings will also shape the relationship between men and women in the church (vv. 13-15). In the ancient Roman world of Corinth, young men shear off their girlish locks at puberty to define their masculinity and signal their preparation for marriage. For a Corinthian to wear his hair long indicates a denial of his masculinity or an aversion to marriage and suggests homosexuality. Long hair identifies a woman. Short hair identifies a man. That is the cultural standard in Corinth in the first-century Roman world. Consequently, for Christians to fly in the face of this deeply ingrained understanding of the distinction between sexes will create confusion among the pagans as to what the church stands for.

This passage does not imply that women should not lead in worship. It simply addresses how they should conduct themselves when they do lead in worship. And this passage does not exalt men in worship. It simply addresses how men should conduct themselves so that they do not exalt themselves. This passage does not define the relationship between men and women and their relative roles in the church. Instead, in this passage, Paul addresses our attitudes toward worship and how the pagan culture around us will understand it. What we see in the passage from a distance, with a cursory look through the spectacles of twenty-first-century life in America, and what we see in the passage up close, with a more in-depth look through the spectacles of first-century life in Corinth, are totally different.

This passage intersects with our lives today at two points. To begin with, our text reminds us that *the purpose of worship is not to exalt us but to exalt Christ*. The principle Old Testament term translated "worship" is the word *shachah*, which means to bow down or to prostrate oneself before someone. The principle New Testament term translated "worship" is the word *proskuneo*, which means to kiss the hand toward someone or to prostrate oneself before someone in reverence. To worship God therefore means to bow down before him and to prostrate ourselves before him in reverence. Consequently, if we seek to exalt ourselves in worship instead of exalting God, like the men in first-century Corinth who paraded before God with their togas, Paul's challenge will reverberate across the centuries: "Don't do that. Quit showing off. Quit following the pattern of the pagans. Your glory is not in you; your glory is in the fact that you have been made for God and belong to God." The purpose of worship is to exalt God, not us.

In addition, our text reminds us that *the purpose of worship is not to exercise our rights but to present to the world an inviting image of what it means to be a part of the family of God*. One writer expresses this truth in these words: "The church at the beginning of the twenty-first century finds itself in desperate need of a theology of 'otherness.'"[2] I think he is right. The church is not about us; it is about reaching the world with the gospel. It is about extending the family of God until it includes all the peoples of the world. Consequently, if we today seek to shape the life of the church around our needs and our desires and our rights, like the women in first-century Corinth who discard their veils in a demonstration of their newfound freedom, Paul's challenge will reverberate across the centuries: "Don't do that. Quit following the pattern of the pagans. Your freedom is not the freedom to do what you want; you are only free to do what brings glory to God and what extends the work of the kingdom." The purpose of the church is to take the gospel to the world.

Notes

1. Ian McEwan, *Atonement* (New York: Anchor Books, 2001).

2. Robert N. Nash, *An 8-Track Church in a CD World* (Macon GA: Smyth & Helwys Publishing, 1997) 41.

28

Experiencing True Fellowship in the Church

1 Corinthians 11:17–34

One of the most moving books I have read in recent years is *Same Kind of Different as Me,* written by Ron Hall and Denver Moore. Ron and Deborah Hall accumulated a great deal of wealth, but then, as Christians, they desired to move from success to significance. As an outlet for their desire to serve God and help people, they became involved with the homeless in the Union Gospel Mission in Ft. Worth. Through their involvement in the people's lives and their unconditional love, they literally transformed the homeless community and the city of Ft. Worth. This book is the story of their transformational love.

The story is told, in part, through the words of one of the homeless men, Denver Moore. Denver was born in rural Louisiana in January 1937 and grew up in poverty with his uncle and aunt who were sharecroppers. When he finally left home, he started down a pathway that led him to a ten-year stint in Angola Prison. When he got out of prison in 1976, he drifted over to Ft. Worth, and for the next twenty-two years he lived as a homeless person on the streets of that city. There in Ft. Worth, his life intersected with the lives of Ron and Deborah Hall when they began their move from success to significance. Initially he violently resisted their help, but eventually their love and persistence broke down the barriers of distrust constructed through a lifetime of mistreatment and misery. The power of God's love demonstrated through the lives of Ron and Deborah Hall transformed this previously incorrigible drifter and released his natural giftedness that had been neutralized by his choices and circumstances for so long.[1]

The book connects with the reader because of the picture of unconditional love depicted by the main characters. This love creates a life-transforming fellowship in which everyone is accepted and loved. Unfortunately, such fellowship does not always characterize the church, either in the twenty-first century or in the first century. For example, the church in Corinth experiences divisions that rend the fellowship, marginalize some of the members, and dilute the unconditional love and unparalleled acceptance that should characterize the church. Surprisingly, these divisions erupt when the Corinthian church participates in the one activity that should draw them together, the celebration of the Lord's Supper. Let us explore this crisis that disrupts the fellowship of the church as the Corinthian Christians attempt to contextualize the gospel in their culture.

In first-century Corinth, the church does not meet in buildings like our church buildings today that are constructed specifically for worship. Instead, the church meets in private homes. In first-century Corinth, the dining room of a typical house seats about ten people who recline at the table for the meal. The other guests have to sit or stand in an area we might call an atrium, which provides space for another thirty or forty people. The host of these gatherings is usually one of the wealthier members of the church who has a house adequate for such meetings. Understandably, these hosts invite their friends to sit in the dining room area, while the lower-status members of the church have to congregate in the larger atrium. The higher-status guests in the dining room usually receive better food than the others, similar to the better meals served to people in the first-class section of an airplane.

When the church in Corinth comes together, they follow the procedure commonly practiced in the city. The wealthy Christian who hosts the gathering has his friends in the special seats in the dining room, and the other Christians, those of the lower classes, gather in the atrium area. Instead of sharing the food, the wealthy members eat all the good food themselves and leave nothing for the poorer members. These wealthy church leaders therefore perpetuate in the church the same class-consciousness and the same divisions that characterize the world.

Is Paul pleased with this practice? Does Paul approve of such actions? Absolutely not. Instead, Paul exclaims, *I have no praise for you* (v. 17). He says, *Your meetings do more harm than good* (v. 17). And he complains, *When you come together, it is not the Lord's Supper you eat* (v. 20). Paul's response provides a warning not only to the Corinthian church of the first century but also to every church today. "Whenever we perpetuate in the church the distinction between the insiders and outsiders that is a part of the world's understanding," Paul warns, "we are no longer being the church."

Why do we do that? Why do we perpetuate the same divisions in the church? Sometimes our pride causes us to perpetuate those distinctions in the church. Our pride whispers in our ear that we are after all better than other people, and we then try to confirm our superiority in the social structure around us.

At other times our lack of self-worth causes us to perpetuate those distinctions in the church. A mother found her little daughter crying because a poor family down the street had moved away. The mother told her, "Honey, I didn't know you cared so much for those children."

The little girl explained, "That's not why I'm crying. I'm crying because, now that they are gone, there is nobody on the block that I am better than." Sometimes the need to prove we are better than someone causes us to establish in-groups and out-groups in society and place ourselves in the in-group. Why do we perpetuate the in-group and out-group distinctions in the church? The primary answer is that we have not yet been captured by the attitude and spirit of Christ.

I think this is why Paul pulls into the text, at this point, what he had been taught concerning the special communion meal Jesus instituted on the last night of his life (vv. 23-25).

At this special meal we know now as the Lord's Supper, Jesus demonstrates the attitude that characterizes his life—an attitude of humility, acceptance, and inclusive love. *This is my body, which is for you*, Jesus says (v. 24). He never looks out for his own welfare. Instead, he continuously gives himself for the welfare of humanity, ultimately going to the cross and giving up his very body for us. This self-giving attitude of Jesus stands in direct opposition to the in-group, privileged, I'm-better-than-you-are mentality of the world. So Paul warns the Corinthian Christians, *When you gather at the Lord's table to take the communion meal, but at the same time maintain these divisions of the world, you are not displaying the spirit of Christ. Therefore, it is not the Lord's Supper you eat* (vv. 20-21). Jesus' self-giving conduct, represented by the communion meal, condemns the self-centered conduct of the Corinthian Christians that is demonstrated in their behavior at the meal.

What should the Corinthians do? Paul adds, *Therefore, whoever eats the bread or drinks the cup of the Lord in an unworthy manner will be guilty of sinning against the body and blood of the Lord. A man ought to examine himself before he eats of the bread and drinks of the cup* (vv. 27-28). By "unworthy," Paul does not refer to our sin as if to suggest that we have to be without sin to partake of the Lord's Supper. All of us are sinners. If we have to be sinless before we are worthy to partake of the Lord's Supper, none of us will ever be worthy. By "unworthy," Paul has in mind our attitude toward each other. In effect, he suggests, "When we partake of the Lord's Supper with an attitude of disdain toward other Christians because we think we are better than they are, then we are profaning the very meaning of the Lord's Supper." In that case, we are not being the church or displaying the attitude of Christ.

Two attitudes, then, clash in Corinthian church of the first century. On the one hand we see *philadelphia*—love for our brothers and sisters, love for those from a common social setting, love for those who are like us. Even the world displays this brotherly love. On the other hand we see *philoxenia*—love for the stranger, love for those with whom we have little in common, love for those who are different. That is the unique kind of love to be displayed by those in the church.

In our text, Paul provides a picture of what *philadelphia* looks like, the kind of love for those who are like us. Let me provide one picture of what *philoxenia* looks like that I heard in a sermon several years ago. The First Baptist Church of a university town is a formal church with rich traditions and a membership that includes the most respected and wealthiest citizens of the city. The members of the church gather faithfully every Sunday in their small but ornate sanctuary to worship their God. But then, one day, a young college student named Bill enters the sanctuary. He has no shoes. He wears jeans and a T-shirt. Earrings pierce both ears, tattoos decorate both arms, and his hair sticks out in every direction. The service is already in progress as Bill moves down the center aisle looking for a seat. Most pews are full, and no one offers to get up and let him sit on their pew, so he keeps moving toward the front of the church. Arriving at the first pew and still finding no seat available, he sprawls out on the carpet. That often happens in discussion groups on campus, but never has it happened at First Baptist Church. Tension pervades the congregation.

At that point, an old deacon in his eighties, with silver-gray hair and an expensive suit, stands up and begins to walk with the aid of his cane slowly toward the front of the church. Everyone whispers, "Well, you can't blame him for what he is going to do," or "How can you expect a man of his age to understand some college kid on the floor?" It takes a long time for the man to reach the front of the sanctuary where the student sits on the floor. The pastor stops speaking. Most of the members of the congregation stop breathing. Only the clicking sound of the man's cane as he moves inexorably to the front of the church shatters the silence. When he gets to where the young student sits on the floor, the deacon drops his cane to the floor and, with great difficulty, he lowers himself and sits next to Bill so that he will not sit on the floor alone. When the pastor finally gains control of his emotions, he says, "What I'm about to preach, you will never remember. But what you have just seen, you will never forget." That is *philoxenia*—love of the stranger.

Philadelphia, the spirit of the world, or *philoxenia*, the spirit of Christ—which will prevail in our churches today?

Note

1. Ron Hall and Denver Moore, *Same Kind of Different as Me* (Nashville: Thomas Nelson, 2006).

29

The Gifts of the Spirit

1 Corinthians 12:1–11

Now about spiritual gifts, brothers, I do not want you to be ignorant (v. 1). The statement with which Paul begins the twelfth chapter of his first letter to the Corinthians is as relevant to the church today as any statement made in the New Testament, for no element of the church's life creates as much confusion as the question concerning spiritual gifts. "Do I have a spiritual gift? If so, where does it come from? What should I do with it? And how can I discover what it is?" I hear these questions, in one form or another, nearly every week from a fellow church member. Paul provides some answers to those questions in our text for this chapter.

The foundational question most Christians ask about this issue is, "Do I have a spiritual gift?" The answer to that question is, "Yes. Every Christian has a spiritual gift." That assurance grows out of the pivotal verse in the passage where Paul declares, *Now to each one the manifestation of the Spirit is given* (v. 7). What is this "manifestation of the Spirit"? The answer comes in the preceding verses where Paul explains, *There are different kinds of gifts, but the same Spirit. There are different kinds of service, but the same Lord. There are different kinds of working, but the same God works all of them in all men* (vv. 4-6). Each one of us has been given a spiritual gift. Even if we have not matured as Christians through the shaping of spiritual disciplines, we still have a spiritual gift. Even if the fruit of the Spirit, described in Galatians 5, is not clearly evident in our lives, we still have a spiritual gift. A spiritual gift is the ability to perform some ministry for God, and the New Testament repeatedly declares that every Christian has at least one spiritual gift. For example, in Ephesians 4:7 the Bible says, "But to each one of us grace has been given as Christ apportioned it." First Peter 4:10 concurs: "Each one should use whatever gift he has received to serve others," implying that everyone has received a gift. In 1 Corinthians 7:7, the Bible says, "But each man has his own gift from God." Every Christian has a spiritual gift.

This truth rules out self-depreciation and self-pity in the body of Christ, for it means every Christian is important. We cannot complain that we do not have a spiritual gift, for the Bible says we do. We cannot crawl back into some corner and pout because we do not think we can do anything significant in God's kingdom, for the Bible says we can. God distributes spiritual gifts to every member of the body of Christ.

Not everybody has the same gift. In verse 4, Paul explains, *There are different kinds of gifts.* In verse 20, Paul adds, "As it is, there are many parts, but one body." Every Christian has a spiritual gift, but the Bible makes it clear that the Holy Spirit distributes these gifts to believers with a rich diversity. In verses 8-10, Paul mentions nine specific gifts: wisdom, knowledge, wonder-working faith, healings, miracles, prophecy, tongues, and the interpretation of tongues. This list is not exhaustive or exclusive but illustrative of the variety of the gifts the Spirit gives to different Christians.

This conviction concerning spiritual gifts means there is no one all-gift Christian—one Christian in whose life all the gifts are found. This conviction also signifies that there is no one all-Christian gift—one gift for which every Christian should strive. God loves variety in his church. That is why, through his Spirit, God distributes the spiritual gifts *just as he determines* (v. 11). Every Christian has a spiritual gift.

That leads to a second question: "Where do these spiritual gifts come from?" Paul answers that question in our text:

> To one there is given through the Spirit the message of wisdom, to another the message of knowledge by means of the same Spirit, to another faith by the same Spirit, to another gifts of healing by that one Spirit . . . . All these are the work of one and the same Spirit, and he gives them to each one, just as he determines. (vv. 8-11)

These spiritual gifts come from God. They are gifts. We do not develop our own spiritual gifts. We do not divvy up these spiritual gifts according to our whims. These spiritual gifts come from God, and they are given to us through his Spirit.

If every Christian has a spiritual gift and if these have been distributed to us by the Spirit, a third question arises: "What should we do with these spiritual gifts?" The Bible says we have been given these spiritual gifts so that we can be a part of God's kingdom work. *Now to each one the manifestations of the Spirit is given for the common good,* Paul explains (v. 7).

In the last part of the chapter, Paul uses the body to illustrate this point. Paul imagines what it would be like if different parts of the body begin to belittle the importance of other parts of the body. Can you imagine the hand saying to the foot, "Here foot, catch this baseball"? When the hand drops the baseball, it bounces off the foot and rolls away. And the hand says to the foot, "You are totally worthless. You can't even catch a baseball." Can you imagine the nose saying to the ear, "Do you smell that barbecue on the grill"? The ear says in response, "I don't smell anything." And the nose says to the ear, "You are worthless. You can't even smell." Can you imagine the different parts of the body carrying on that kind of conversation with each other? Of course not.

Instead, the nose says to the ear, "I don't care if you can smell. I just want you to hear." The hand says to the foot, "I don't care if you can catch a baseball. I just want you to be able to move the body from one place to another." The heart doesn't say to the liver, "You're not beating," or the eye to the big toe, "You're not looking." Every part of the body has a distinct function in the overall working of the body. Paul applies that analogy of the body to the church and declares, "Now you are the body of Christ, and each one of you is a part of it" (12:27). With the spiritual gifts God has given to Christians, each of us can play a part in God's kingdom work. We can be a part of the body of Christ as it functions in the world.

So how then can we discover our spiritual gift(s)? Let me offer these suggestions.

The first step is *to understand what the gifts are.* Paul offers two lists of these gifts in 1 Corinthians 12, one in verses 8-10 and another in verses 28-30. These lists are supplemented by other lists in Romans 12, Ephesians 4, and 1 Peter 4. We must remember that these lists are not exhaustive but exemplary. To understand what the gifts are, we need to study these passages. We need to analyze ways in which God has gifted people in the past. He has gifted some to teach, and to others he has given the gift of helps. He has gifted some to preach, and to others he has given the gift of craftsmanship. We need to expand our minds with the possible gifts with which God can endow an individual Christian. That is the place to start.

The second step is *to discover what inspires us.* What do we enjoy doing? What are we good at? What touches us in our inner being and appeals to us to do something about it? God does not always reveal his will to us in spectacular manifestations but sometimes in the normal, commonsense experience of life through the things that appeal to us. We need to follow our passion, and then we will probably be on a pathway that will lead to the discovery of our spiritual gift(s).

The third step is *to seek input from others.* One of the most marvelous results of Christian fellowship is that someone else often sees something in us that we do not see ourselves. We might call it "finding our life cue." In our association with others, they will often find a life cue in our lives and draw it out, helping us find our gifts.

The fourth step is *to act on our opportunities.* Some people are caught up in the paralysis of analysis. That is, they are so caught up in studying the lists of gifts and looking for their gift and talking about their gift that they never do anything for God. They spend all their time analyzing themselves. We do not have to discover our specific gift before we act. Rather, as we act in Christian love, as we minister to other members of the body of Christ, our gift or gifts will become increasingly clear to us and to others. As we look back at our past ministries in Christ's name, we will often discover what our gift is. In other words, we will discover what God has gifted us to do by doing what God has given us to do. As we go through the doors of opportunity God places before us and serve others in Jesus' name, we will discover more and more about what our spiritual gifts are.

To his young friend Timothy, Paul gives this admonition: "I remind you to fan into flame the gift of God, which is in you" (2 Tim 1:6). Our text presents the same challenge to each of us. God has distributed a rich diversity of gifts throughout the membership of our churches. He gives us these gifts to build up the church, to produce fellowship, and to extend the witness of Christ. Therefore, we need to fan into flame the gift of God that is in us and dedicate it to the service of God through his church and in our community. In doing so, we will be equipped to contextualize the gospel in the culture around us.

30

Spiritual Gifts and the Church

1 Corinthians 12:12-31

In 1941 C. S. Lewis penned one of the cleverest Christian books ever written, *The Screwtape Letters*. Lewis's book contains letters Screwtape, a senior devil, allegedly writes to a junior devil to teach him the proper strategy for enticing human beings to yield to temptation. According to these letters, Satan does not use obvious things to lead us astray. Instead, he tempts us in unexpected ways, at unexpected times, and using unexpected objects. Satan often distorts something good like prayer, success at work, the adoration of friends, or even the church into an instrument of our downfall.[1]

Satan's approach, revealed in C. S. Lewis's book, probably explains a strange phenomenon I notice in Paul's letter to the Corinthian Christians. Paul writes this letter to Christians who are attempting to establish the church in the materialistic, pagan city of Corinth, an undertaking plagued with numerous problems. Paul addresses these problems in this letter we know as 1 Corinthians. Yet I have always been perplexed by the amount of space Paul gives to these various problems.

For example, conflict often erupts in the church at Corinth. Paul deals with that problem in one chapter. Immorality also permeates the church. One man even takes his father's wife as his wife. Paul deals with that problem in one chapter. The Corinthians become confused about how to live together as husband and wife and wonder whether to get married in the first place. This issue affects everything they do. Paul deals with that problem in one chapter. The Christians at Corinth create dissension every time they observe the Lord's Supper, turning what should be a sacred moment into an opportunity for personal gratification. Again, Paul deals with this problem in one chapter. The Christians at Corinth seem to be confused about the resurrection of Jesus and how that relates to their own future resurrection. Paul responds to this thorny theological issue in one chapter. These are all major problems, and yet Paul deals with each of them in a chapter or less.

However, when he addresses the presence and manifestation of spiritual gifts, an issue that seems rather innocuous compared to these other issues, Paul devotes three whole chapters to the problem. Why does he do that? Spiritual gifts are good. They should not be a problem. Why then does Paul spend only one chapter on these apparently major problems facing the church at Corinth but then three chapters on the issue of spiritual gifts? C. S. Lewis's insight provides an answer. In this area where the Corinthians least expect Satan to stir things up among them, he will most certainly be at work. Satan strategically uses unexpected times and seemingly innocuous things to disrupt the work of the church. Consequently, Paul gives extra space in his letter to the Corinthian Christians—three chapters, in fact—to the issue of spiritual gifts.

In the opening verses of 1 Corinthians 12, Paul answers three basic questions about spiritual gifts. Question 1 is, "Do I have a spiritual gift?" The answer to that question is, "Yes. If you are a Christian, you have a spiritual gift." Question 2 is, "Where do these gifts come from?" The answer to that question is, "God gives them to us through his Spirit." Question 3 is, "What do we do with these spiritual gifts?" The answer to that question is, "We are to use them for the common good. That is, we are to use them for the work of God's kingdom." I added a fourth question in the last chapter: "How can we discover our spiritual gifts?" I provided several answers to that question. We can succinctly summarize Paul's declaration in the opening verses of 1 Corinthians 12 concerning spiritual gifts in a simple statement: God can use us right now, where we are, with what we have to do his kingdom work.

That wonderful news should encourage every Christian. Even if we are not "important" in the eyes of the world, we have value in the eyes of God. God can and will use us to accomplish something in his kingdom work. However, Satan takes that truth about spiritual gifts, which is good and should be uplifting, and twists it around until it becomes a source of conflict and confusion in the church, and he usually does this in one of two ways.

On the one hand, Satan twists the positive affirmation that each of us is valuable to God into the unhealthy assumption that some of us are more valuable than others. As a result, he distorts the healthy sense of self-worth that comes from the recognition of our gifts into an unhealthy sense of self-importance that comes from the exaltation of our gifts.

Paul witnesses that phenomenon in the church at Corinth. Some members of the church flaunt their spiritual gifts, and as a result other members of the church feel despised or even ostracized because they do not have the same spiritual gifts. Instead of reflecting the diversity God wants in his church, these contrasting spiritual gifts provide the seedbed for division. Paul addresses this problem with the instructive image of the church as the body of Christ (vv. 14-20).

What does Paul mean with this metaphor? He reminds the Corinthians that the church does not have one all-Christian gift, one gift for which every Christian should strive, one gift that marks its holder as superior to other Christians. Instead, God distributes a diversity of gifts to the members of the body of Christ, and sometimes the gifts that seem least important to us are the ones God uses in extraordinary ways.

Let me give one example. A number of years ago, a Baptist Student Union sponsored a rally on the university campus at the beginning of the school year and invited as the special guest Paul Anderson, who at that time was known as the strongest man in the world. He performed feats of strength—like lifting a table with ten people on it—and then after the people "oohed" and "ahhed," he shared his Christian testimony. Then he invited people to come forward and commit their lives to Christ. On this particular night, a young lady in a wheelchair, a paraplegic, moved her chair to the front to make a decision. Then another young lady who was standing behind her made a decision as well. One of the counselors asked the second girl what part of Paul Anderson's testimony persuaded her to make her decision. She explained, "I don't know what Paul Anderson said. I really didn't pay that much attention to him. But when this girl"—and she pointed to the girl in the wheelchair—"decided that Christ would accept her, then I decided that maybe Christ would accept me as well." The strongest man in the world stood before the crowd, but God used a paraplegic in a wheelchair to bring this young college student to Christ. Why? God sometimes uses the gifts that seem unimportant to us in extraordinary ways.

Each of us is valuable to God. That is certainly true. Yet we must not allow Satan to twist that positive affirmation into the unhealthy assumption that some of us have more value to God than others. If we do, then we will lose the diversity with which God has gifted his body.

Satan tries to twist our understanding of spiritual gifts in another way. He twists the positive affirmation that each of us can contribute to God's kingdom work into the unhealthy assumption that only our contribution is important. As a result, a healthy sense of interdependence shifts into an unhealthy sense of individuality.

That too happens in the church at Corinth. Some members of the church exalt their contribution to the church, and as a result other members of the church feel neglected or ignored because they cannot make the same contribution. Instead of everyone working together, some Christians feel they can do the work of the church by themselves. Paul addresses this problem in 1 Corinthians 12:21-26. In his response, Paul reminds the Corinthians that the church does not have any one all-gift Christian, one Christian who possesses every spiritual gift, one Christian who can, by himself or herself, accomplish the work of God's kingdom. Instead, God creates the body of Christ in such a way that we are all dependent on each other. No one of us can make it alone.

Maya Angelou captures this truth in one of her poems that is simply titled "Alone." Here are some of the lines of the poem.

> Lying, thinking
> Last night
> How to find my soul a home
> Where water is not thirsty
> And bread loaf is not stone.
> I came up with one thing
> And I don't believe I'm wrong
> That nobody,
> But nobody
> Can make it out here alone.
>
> Alone, all alone
> Nobody, but nobody
> Can make it out here alone.
>
> Now if you listen closely
> I'll tell you what I know
> Storm clouds are gathering
> The wind is gonna blow
> The race of man is suffering
> And I can hear the moan,
> 'Cause nobody

But nobody,
Can make it out here alone.

Alone, all alone
Nobody, but nobody
Can make it out here alone.[2]

Paul pronounces that same testimony about the Christian life. That message permeates this description of the church in 1 Corinthians 12: "Nobody, but nobody can make it out here alone." Why? Each of us is a part of the body of Christ, and God creates us to work in interdependence with each other.

Each of us can contribute to the kingdom of God. That is true. Yet we must not allow Satan to twist that positive affirmation into the unhealthy assumption that only we can make a contribution. If we do, then we will lose the interdependence that is essential to the effective working of the church. Only when we recognize the importance of every gift and only when we work together as a unit can we function as the body of Christ.

Someone surmised that the world is composed of three categories of people: the plus/plus people, the plus/minus people, and the minus/minus people. The plus/plus people say, "I can do it and you can do it. So together, let's get it done." The plus/minus people say, "I can do it, but you can't do it. So get out of the way and I'll get it done." The minus/minus people say, "I can't do it, and you can't do it. So whoever brought it up in the first place?"

Where does the church fit in those three categories? Satan tempts us to put the church in the third category. "The church can't really make a difference in the world," Satan says. "You're just a bunch of nobodies. The world is too big and the church is too small." Paul deals with that temptation in the first eleven verses of 1 Corinthians 12. He reminds us that even if we appear to be a bunch of nobodies in the eyes of the world, the Holy Spirit has nevertheless gifted us and empowered us. Because of those gifts, God can use each one of us right now, where we are, to do his kingdom work. Therefore, the church does not fit in that third category.

Satan then tempts us to put the church in the second category. "Some people in the church might be important, and they might get some things done," Satan will concede. "But most people in the church are too weak and too insignificant, and for them to think they can really make any difference in the world is a pipe dream." Paul deals with that temptation in our text for this chapter. All of us in the church have value because the Holy Spirit has given to each of us the unique gift God wants us to have, and God loves variety in his church. Consequently, no one can do the work of the church alone. It takes all of us working together. Therefore, the church does not fit in the second category.

So where does the church fit? It fits in the first category. Because God has gifted each of us, because each gift is important, and because each of us can accomplish something for God, this should be the mantra of the church: "I can do it, and you can do it. So together, let's get it done." The church is a group of plus/plus people who, out of the diversity of our giftedness and in the interdependence of our actions, function as the body of Christ. Consequently, we have everything we need to contextualize the gospel in our culture.

Notes

1. C. S. Lewis, *The Screwtape Letters* (New York: A Touchstone Book, 1961).

2. Maya Angelou, *Poems* (New York: Bantam Books, 1986) 69–70.

31

What's Love Got to Do with It?

1 Corinthians 13:1-13

I can still remember how excited I was. I thought it was a coup for our church. We were hosting a youth rally for Escambia County. Hundreds of young people from all over the county would be at our church, the First Baptist Church of Pensacola. We had enlisted one of the most popular Christian singers of the day to do a concert. I will not mention his name for reasons that will become apparent. We sent out massive communications to the community. Dozens of other local churches joined in the effort. On the night of the concert, young people squeezed into every nook and cranny of the church sanctuary, overflowing the pews and even sitting on the floor. I scheduled a time just before the concert to meet with the artist. I invited the key youth leaders and those who helped organize the event to join us. I wanted us to pray for God's blessings on our evening. I wanted us all to be spiritually prepared for what God was going to do in that concert. As it turned out, this was one of the most disappointing meetings in which I have been involved. To use the word "prima donna" to speak of this Christian musician would be the nicest possible description I could use. More appropriate words would be demanding, condescending, obnoxious, and arrogant. This man was certainly gifted, and he is still a popular artist today. However, I was jarred by the contrast between his attempt to use his gifts for the Lord and the blatantly unchristian spirit in which he used those gifts. This contrast between his performance and his persona raises an important question: "What is wrong with this picture?"

The same thing happens in the church at Corinth as these first-century Christians exercise their spiritual gifts. Even though these Christians recognize the diversity and interdependence of these gifts (the subject we covered in the last chapter), they forget something more important. They lose sight of the centrality of love in the Christian life. The key element of the Christian life, according to the New Testament, is not how we perform as Christians but how we treat other people. Jesus affirms the centrality of love when he tells his disciples on the last night of his life, "By this all men will know that you are my disciples, if you love one another" (John 13:35). Paul agrees. As a result, right in the middle of his discussion on spiritual gifts, Paul inserts this remarkable chapter on love.

Our initial response to 1 Corinthians 13 might be to ask the question raised by Tina Turner's hit song back in the 1980s: "What's love got to do with it?" The answer to the question is *everything*. The Corinthian Christians have become so enamored with spiritual gifts, so caught up in the glamour and excitement of performing miracles and giving prophecies and speaking in tongues, that they forget that the essential characteristic of the Christian life—the core value of the church—is not the exercise of our spiritual gifts but the expression of our love for one another. Paul develops that thought in one of the most beloved portions of Scripture.

The citizens of first-century Corinth consider five things most important in life: oratory, prophecy, miracle working, philanthropy, and martyrdom. Paul identifies these five things in the opening verses of this thirteenth chapter not to suggest that love is better than these five things but to confirm that even if we have all five of those things but do not have love, we really have nothing at all:

> If I speak in the tongues of men and of angels, but have not love, I am only a resounding gong or a clanging cymbal. If I have the gift of prophecy and can fathom all mysteries and all knowledge, and if I have a faith that can move mountains, but have not love, I am nothing. If I give all I possess to the poor and surrender my body to the flames, but have not love, I gain nothing. (vv. 1-3)

If Paul wrote this letter to our churches in the twenty-first century, he probably would not allude to the five elements he mentions to the Corinthians: oratory, prophecy, miracle working, philanthropy, and martyrdom. He might, instead, address the five issues that dominate our thinking today: what we accomplish, what we say, what we know, what we believe, and what we give. Nevertheless, he would apply the same principle. *What we accomplish* is not the central element in the Christian life, he would affirm, for success without service is absolutely useless. *What we say* is not the central element in the Christian life, for saying the right thing without doing the right thing is absolutely useless. *What we know* is not the central element in the Christian life, for knowledge that is not used to improve the lives of those around us is absolutely useless. *What we believe* is not the central element in the Christian life, for unless our theology is translated into the biography of our lives, it is absolutely useless. And *what we give* is not the central element in the Christian life, for giving to others or to Christ with reluctance in our heart misses the whole point of giving. If we accomplish every personal goal, always say just the right thing, learn everything we can learn, are orthodox in our beliefs, and give sacrificially to the church, but do not love people, then we have absolutely nothing.

So what's love got to do with it? The answer to that question is *everything*. Only if we love as Jesus calls us to love will we live as Jesus calls us to live.

But what does it mean to love as Jesus called us to love? In the middle part of this extraordinary chapter, Paul highlights two qualities of authentic Christian love (v. 4).

To begin with, Paul tells us that real Christian love is a self-initiated response to life. To use Paul's words, "Love is patient." "Patient" does not mean simply holding on in the midst of difficulties. It also means moving forward in the midst of opposition. No matter what others do to us, we are to continue to love them. Why? Because the actions of others do not determine our love. Our love flows naturally out of our commitment to Christ. Our love is not determined by what others do to us. It is instead determined by what Christ has done for us. Christian love is a self-initiated response to life.

Let me give one illustration of this self-initiating quality of love. A sixteen-year-old girl named Jennifer, a middle child, exists in the uncomfortable tension between an older sister who excels in everything and a younger brother whom everybody loves. Beginning in junior high, Jennifer begins to pull away from the family, falls into frequent delinquency from school, and eventually attempts to take her own life with an overdose of pills. Her mother finds her when she comes home from work. Jennifer revives enough to explain to her mother what she has done. The mother rushes her daughter to the hospital, where the medical team pumps out her stomach and saves her life. Counseling follows, but Jennifer continues in her delinquent activities. One night Jennifer's mother awakes while it is still dark and begins to pray. In her prayer time, God prompts her to reach out to Jennifer again. The next morning, as Jennifer dresses to go to school, her mother sticks her head in her door and says, "Jennifer, I don't know why you have been going through all the things you have, but I want you to know—there is nothing you can do to ever make me stop loving you."[1] Why does she say that to Jennifer? Because she is Jennifer's mother, and the natural response of a mother is to love her child regardless of what she has done.

Paul makes the same point in our text concerning Christian love. We are to love others because it is the nature of a Christian to love. No matter what others do, we still love them because our love is not determined by our relationship to them. It is determined by our relationship to Christ. Christian love is a self-initiated response to life. "Love is patient," Paul says.

Paul identifies a second quality of Christian love. He affirms that Christian love is a life-transforming response to life. To use Paul's words, *Love is kind* (v. 4). The J. B. Phillips' translation has Paul say, "Love looks for a way of being constructive." Christian love expresses itself. It acts. It reaches out. It lifts up. It encourages. Christian love always looks for a way of being constructive.

Let me give one illustration of this dimension of love. In a YMCA basketball league for middle school boys, two teams face each other, the first-place team and the last-place team. The first-place team plays like a well-oiled machine. They run up and down the court from the beginning of the game to the end. They destroy whomever they play. The other team stands in stark contrast to that efficient team. They barely compete against any team, much less this league-leading team. The first-place team literally blows the last-place team out of the gym, leading by some fifty points going into the last quarter. In YMCA basketball, everyone on each team must get a chance to play. So at the start of the fourth quarter, with the game far out of reach, both coaches begin to substitute freely. The subs for the first-place team continue to run and play just as magnificently as the starters. Finally, with about four minutes to play, the clock stops on an out-of-bounds play, and the coach of the last-place team puts in his last sub, a boy named Jimmy. Everyone can immediately tell that Jimmy is not like the other boys on the court. While the teams race one way for the basket, Jimmy moves the other direction. By the time he turns around, the rest of the players have reversed their direction.

At one point, however, both Jimmy and the teams go in the same direction and somebody accidentally throws the ball to Jimmy. Everything halts. The officials freeze. The crowd hushes. All the players stop where they are, and the members of this great defensive team, the pride of their coach for not allowing more than ten points per game to be scored, stand still and drop their hands to their sides. Jimmy turns the ball in his hands a couple of times, looks at the basket, takes two or three steps without dribbling, and shoots. He misses. Someone retrieves the ball and hands it back to Jimmy. Still no one moves. Jimmy turns the ball in his hands again, looks at the basket, takes two or three steps without dribbling, and shoots. The ball hits the rim and bounces in. A roar erupts from the crowd. Jimmy jumps up and down with joy. There is not a dry eye in the gym. Suddenly, the game continues with both teams racing up and down the court until the final buzzer.[2]

When, in the rush and busyness of life, we are willing to stop for a minute and reach out a hand of compassion to someone in need, that is Christian love. Christian love is not just a feeling. It is not just words. It is something we do. Love is a life-transforming response to life. "Love looks for a way of being constructive," Paul says.

The central question in the Christian life is simply this: Do I genuinely care for other people? We have nothing and we are nothing without that. Only if we love as Jesus calls us to love will we live as Jesus calls us to live.

Notes

1. Bill Blackburn, *What You Should Know about Suicide* (Waco TX: Word Books, 1982) 115–16.

2. Steven E. Burt, "Taking Time to Love," *Pulpit Digest* 61/450 (July/August 1981): 54–55.

32

The Gift of Tongues

1 Corinthians 14:1–25

Confusion and division reign in the worship services of the Corinthian church. At the heart of the problem is an inordinate attention given to speaking in tongues, or glossolalia (v. 23). What is glossolalia? It can mean speaking in a language that one does not know but that others do know. This seems to be what happens at Pentecost. The Bible says, "All of them were filled with the Holy Spirit and began to speak in other tongues as the Spirit enabled them" (Acts 2:3). In response to this phenomenon, members in the audience reply, "We hear them declaring the wonders of God in our own tongues!" (Acts 2:11). Glossolalia can also mean speaking in an ecstatic language, a spontaneous utterance of incomprehensive and seemingly random vocal sounds. This seems to be the form of glossolalia in the church at Corinth, for Paul warns against expressing the gift of glossolalia in the church unless someone can translate these utterances into intelligible language (v. 13). Glossolalia, speaking in an actual language unknown to the speaker, occurs at Pentecost and results in tremendous growth and blessing for the church. Glossolalia, speaking in an ecstatic language, occurs at Corinth and results in tremendous turmoil and division in the church.

What does the New Testament say about glossolalia or speaking in tongues? Surprisingly, we discover that the New Testament says little about this phenomenon. In only four places does the New Testament refer to this spiritual gift. Luke mentions it in Acts 2 in describing the phenomenon we know as Pentecost. As I mention above, this particular manifestation of tongues is speaking in another language that the person speaking does not know but that others can understand. Luke mentions tongues again in Acts 10:44-46 when Peter takes the gospel to the Gentiles. In describing this event (Acts 11:17), Peter explains that God gave "the same gift" at Caesarea as he had at Pentecost. So this manifestation of tongues also seems to be speaking in a language that the person speaking does not know but that others can understand, as at Pentecost. Luke mentions tongues a third time in Acts 19:6 when Paul shares Christ with a group of John the Baptist's disciples at Ephesus. Luke gives no clue to help us discern whether this manifestation of tongues is speaking in actual languages or speaking with ecstatic utterances. What does seem clear is that each time Luke mentions the phenomenon of tongues in the book of Acts, this manifestation signals another barrier broken down by the gospel and activates the spread of the gospel of Christ to yet another plateau. In each case, the phenomenon of tongues affirms God's approval of what is happening.

Other than these three instances, we find the only other mention of tongues in the letter to the church at Corinth. More significant than the times the gift of tongues *is* mentioned are the times when it *is not* mentioned. The phenomenon of tongues never appears in the life and experience of our Lord Jesus, although the Holy Spirit filled Jesus more than anyone (Luke 3:21). The Gospels never allude to this phenomenon. Arguably the most spiritual book of the New Testament, the Gospel of John, never refers to it. Paul does not include speaking in tongues in the charismatic lists in Romans 12:6-8 and Ephesians 4:11. With the exception of the passages in 1 Corinthians 12–14, Paul never mentions this gift in any of his other epistles.

What can we conclude from this brief survey? The New Testament does not highlight the gift of tongues. Instead, tongues is a rare phenomenon found only in a few places, and as far as we know in only one church, and it was not a spiritual church but a carnal one filled with every problem and disorder. In fact, the outbreak of tongues in the Corinthian church creates such confusion and disorder that Paul gives an entire chapter in his letter to address the issue.

Paul does not disallow the gift of tongues. He allows it as a personal expression of praise to God. However, he limits it as a part of worship in the gathered assembly. In comparison to the gift of prophecy, the gift of tongues comes in a distant second in Paul's estimation. In the opening verses of our text, Paul contrasts tongues and prophecy. Paul acknowledges first of all the different direction of these two gifts. Tongues has an upward direction while prophecy has an outward direction (vv. 1-3). Consequently, exercising the gift of tongues does not provide a word of comfort for the believers or communicate the good news to the unbeliever. The gift of tongues simply edifies the individual believer expressing this gift. In contrast, prophecy is directed to other people and provides "strengthening, encouragement, and comfort" to those who have gathered in the assembly of worship (v. 3).

This distinction places prophecy on a higher level because the New Testament clearly confirms that the ultimate purpose of spiritual gifts is to build up the church. God gives these spiritual gifts not as an adornment for private benefit or as an announcement of certain achievement or as an award to distinguish God's elite. Instead, God distributes these gifts as an anointment for service. First Peter 4:10 puts it like this: "As each one has received a special gift, employ it in serving one another" (NASB). Paul echoes this idea when he tells the Corinthians, "Now to each one the manifestation of the Spirit is given for the common good" (1 Cor 12:7). Likewise, Paul implies in our text for this chapter that we most effectively display our spiritual gifts when we use them to *build up the church* (v. 12). Consequently, when our expression of this gift disrupts the fellowship of the church instead of strengthening it, we are misusing our gift. Likewise, when our expression of this gift discredits other Christians or diminishes their value, we are misusing our gift. The Spirit gave us our spiritual gifts in order to build up the church. Therefore, Paul confirms the superiority of the gift of prophecy over the gift of tongues because of its effect in the church.

Paul expands on the superiority of prophecy to speaking in tongues in the remainder of the chapter. Why is prophecy superior to tongues? First, prophecy supersedes tongues because tongues requires an interpretation and prophecy does not. Therefore, prophecy provides a clearer and more dependable word from the Lord (v. 13). Paul confirms the importance of intelligibility by using the example of musical instruments (v. 7), the call to battle by the trumpet (v. 8), and foreign languages (vv. 9-10). Second, prophecy supersedes tongues because it involves the mind and not just the emotion (vv. 14-15). Therefore, prophecy produces understanding and not just excitement. Third, prophecy supersedes tongues because prophecy more effectively builds up believers (vv. 16-22). Tongues builds up only the one exercising the gift. Fourth, prophecy supersedes tongues because it is a more effective tool in evangelizing the lost (vv. 23-25). Tongues confuses the unbeliever. Prophecy, on the other hand, presents a message that clearly explains God's offer of salvation. Consequently, as one scholar expresses Paul's attitude toward these two gifts, "He allows tongues and interpretation; he prefers prophecy."[1]

Is tongues still a valid spiritual gift today? I will identify three responses.

Charismatic Christians give a resounding affirmative to that question. In fact, charismatic believers often exalt tongues as the pivotal spiritual gift and imply that those who speak in tongues occupy a higher level of spirituality than those who do not. To them, tongues is not only a valid spiritual gift today but is the ultimate spiritual gift. However, in no place does the New Testament identify speaking in tongues as the preeminent spiritual gift.

Is tongues still a valid spiritual gift today? Other Christians give a resounding negative to this question, declaring that God limits the gift of tongues to the first century as a unique sign-gift at that crucial time in Christian history but that is no longer needed or given today. Those holding this position insist that tongues has ceased as a spiritual gift. However, to reach this conclusion we must give more theological significance to Paul's statement in 1 Corinthians 13:8-12 than it really has, and we must presume on the sovereignty of the Holy Spirit who alone distributes these gifts. In addition, such a position ignores the unambiguous references in our text where Paul affirms tongues as a valid spiritual gift. For example, Paul says, *I would like every one of you to speak in tongues* (v. 5). He also clarifies what believers should do if they speak in a tongue (v. 13). And he clearly affirms, *I thank God that I speak in tongues more than all of you* (v. 18). Paul does not disavow speaking in tongues in our text. He simply questions the value of tongues in the gathered assembly of worship because it does not build up the church.

Is tongues still a valid spiritual gift today? A third response is a cautious affirmative. I do not find any clear, strong biblical evidence that the Spirit limited the gift of tongues to one period of Christian history. Therefore, based on my commitment to the Bible as the guide to truth, I have to confirm tongues as a valid spiritual gift today. On the other hand, I do not find any clear, strong biblical evidence that supports the exaltation of tongues or the practice of tongues as we see today in many churches. The suggestion by some scholars that tongues as it was manifest in the Corinthian church distorted the original Pentecostal gift that was given for the purpose of evangelism could also shape our ultimate position on the gift of tongues in the church today. In any case, I reject the resounding yes and the resounding no approaches for what I consider to be the biblical approach: a cautious yes.

The third view seems to fit most comfortably in the context of our text. Paul does not dismiss the practice of speaking in tongues. Instead, he cautions against the pattern and product of speaking in tongues in the gathered assembly of worship. Tongues, not interpreted, will be unintelligible to both believers and nonbelievers. Consequently, it will not edify either group.

What does this mean for us today? First, let me say a negative word. If the gift of tongues is still a valid gift, it must be exercised within the limitations and guidelines of the New Testament. Whenever tongues is exalted as the preeminent gift, elevated to a gift everyone should seek, used to magnify the one who has the gift, or divisive in the church, then we have moved beyond the parameters established by the New Testament.

Let me also offer a positive word. We should not neglect the gifts of the Spirit just because this one gift is sometimes distorted. The Holy Spirit dwells in the life of every believer the moment that person receives Christ, and this indwelling Holy Spirit wants to distribute the appropriate gifts to individual believers in each body of faith so we can do what God wants us to do. We should receive that ministry of the Holy Spirit freely and joyfully and gratefully so that we can be fully equipped to contextualize the gospel in our spiritually hungry world.

Note

1. Gordon D. Fee, *The First Epistle to the Corinthians in The New International Commentary on the New Testament* (Grand Rapids MI: William B. Eerdmans Publishing Company, 1987) 660.

33

Orderly Worship

1 Corinthians 14:26–40

I had only been at the church for a few weeks when I decided to make adjustments in the Sunday morning order of worship. At the time, the church followed the "fill-in-the-blank" approach to worship planning. That is, the church followed the identical order each week: a choral call to worship followed by two hymns, followed by the pastoral prayer, followed by the offertory hymn and the offering, followed by a solo or choir anthem, followed by the sermon, followed by the invitation, followed by the benediction, and concluding with the singing of the doxology. Planning worship consisted of simply penciling in different numbers for the hymns and special music. Even though some of the members considered the order to be sacrosanct, I decided to change it. We started with the reading of the Scripture in which the congregation participated. We bracketed two hymns around a testimony from one of our young adults. We then had a medley of hymns followed by the offering. After my sermon, before the invitation, the choir sang a song that summarized the essence of the message in a beautiful musical rendition, and we ended the service without singing the doxology!

As soon the service was over, an older lady in the congregation accosted me with a red face and her veins bulging on her neck. When she could finally speak, she blurted out, "We didn't sing the doxology. We always sing the doxology. I grew up in this church and as long as I can remember we have sung the doxology at the end of every service. I travel all over the world and whenever I am in another country, I can look at my watch and know that at 12:00 on Sunday morning Pensacola time, as the worship service at First Baptist is drawing to a close, our people are singing the doxology." (I am not making this up! It really happened.) This church member reminded me again—granted, with an extreme example—of the importance of order in worship.

The experience of worship in the Corinthian church disturbs Paul as well, not because the leaders of the church change the order of worship but because inappropriate behavior and uncontrolled outbursts disrupt the worship services. *When you come together,* Paul complains, *everyone has a hymn, or a word of instruction, a revelation, a tongue or an interpretation* (v. 26). Apparently, the worshipers express these gifts all at the same time, producing a cacophony of sound that creates disorder and prevents the worship experience from strengthening the worshipers. So just as Paul earlier warns against unintelligible communication because it fails to edify the worshipers (vv. 1-25), Paul now warns against disorderly worship for the same reason. Disorder in worship prevents the worship experience from building up the believers in the Corinthian church (vv. 26-40).

In this instance, Paul does not contrast the gift of prophecy with the gift of tongues, exalting one gift on a higher plane than the other. Instead, he contrasts the way in which the Corinthian believers use both of these gifts. Instead of using them in an orderly way, they use their spiritual gifts in a way that creates disorder in the church. Again, Paul affirms that the Holy Spirit gives believers spiritual gifts in order to edify or build up the church (v. 26). Yet the Corinthians abuse their spiritual gifts because they misunderstand the purpose of these gifts. Because the gifts are given to edify the church, they must be used in an orderly fashion. Again, Paul sets apart the gift of tongues and the gift of prophecy for special consideration.

He first addresses the use of the gift of tongues (vv. 26-28). When someone speaks in tongues in a worship service, Paul explains, only two or at the most three individuals should participate (v. 27). In addition, whenever someone speaks in tongues in worship, Paul affirms the need for someone to interpret the message. Only then can the congregation benefit from this spiritual gift. If no interpreter is present, Paul commands, the person with the gift of tongues should remain silent. Paul does not devalue the gift of tongues. Instead, he values the need for order in worship.

Paul then addresses the expression of the gift of prophecy (vv. 29-32). Instead of exalting the gift of prophecy over the gift of tongues as he does earlier, Paul places an identical limitation on this gift: only two or three in a service (v. 29). As he recommends the tongues to be interpreted, Paul urges the prophecy to be *weighed carefully.* The Greek word here can mean to judge or simply to discuss. When a worshiper utters a word of prophecy, those who listen ("others") should discuss the prophecy so they can discern its relevance and application to their lives. Interpreters debate whether these "others" are other prophets or simply the other worshipers, but in either case the point is the same. Spontaneous prophetic utterances, given one after another, without taking time to discern the meaning of these utterances, wreak havoc in the worship service.

As Paul roots the earlier admonition against unintelligible communication in the need to offer a word of edification for believers and a word of witness to unbelievers, Paul now roots the admonition against disorder in the nature of God. God, Paul declares, *is not a God of disorder but of peace* (v. 33). In contrast to the deities of the cults who seem to welcome frenzy and disorder in worship, the Christian God welcomes control and order.

Paul turns to another source of disorder in the church, the verbal participation of women in the worship services at Corinth (vv. 33b-35). How are we to understand Paul's command for the women to be silent in the church? Some understand this statement to be an all-inclusive rule for all churches of all times. Consequently, they do not allow women to speak in the church at all. When set in the context of the Corinthian church, Paul's instructions can be understood in one of several ways.

Paul could be concerned about women who speak in tongues, so he forbids the women from using this spiritual gift in the church. Why does he do that? Perhaps the Corinthian women abuse the gift of tongues more than the men, so Paul issues a command to the women to cease doing something that creates disorder in the church. In this case, Paul does not issue a permanent rule against women speaking in the church. Instead, he issues a permanent rule against disorder in the church.

Or Paul could be concerned about women guilty of disruptive speech. Perhaps the women chatter incessantly and ask obtrusive questions that continuously disrupt the worship services. In this case, Paul's concern is not that women speak in church or that they need to be restricted from expressing the gift of tongues. Instead, Paul opposes behavior by the women that creates disorder in the church. If the women cannot control their verbal outbursts in worship, then they need to do their talking at home.

Set in the context of Paul's concern about discerning prophecy (vv. 29-33), perhaps Paul's concern is the attempt of women to discern prophecy. Maybe the wives interject repeated questions to their husbands about the meaning of a prophecy, even questioning the interpretation offered by their husbands, thus embarrassing them and creating tensions in their marriage relationship. In this case, Paul's prohibition is not to women in general but to wives in particular. Concerned with the relationship between husbands and wives, Paul warns the wives to avoid any behavior in public that will strain their private relationship.

The debate concerning the level of participation by women in church continues even in our day. Those who believe God limits women's role in church cite such restrictions as the one Paul makes in our text. Or they quote Paul's instruction to young Timothy: "I do not permit a woman to teach or to have authority over a man; she must be silent" (1 Tim 2:11). Those who believe women can participate in church at an equal level with men also have proof texts to which they point. They note Jesus' unique treatment of women and especially his specific assignment to Mary to proclaim the message of the resurrection (John 20:17). Or they refer to Peter's sermon at Pentecost when he defined this new thing happening in light of Joel's prophecy that God would pour out his Spirit on all people and "your sons and daughters will prophesy" (Joel 2:28). Or they highlight Paul's approval of Priscilla who, along with Aquila, taught Apollos (Act 18:24-26) and led in the church in her house (Rom 16:5). Or they reference Paul's instruction to women earlier in this same Corinthian letter (11:5) where, instead of forbidding women from speaking in church, he simply urges them to cover their heads *when* they prophesy in church (1 Cor 11:5).

As we continue to debate this issue, we need to remember that Paul's primary focus in our text is not what women do in worship but whether or not the Corinthians maintain order in worship so that both believers and nonbelievers can be edified by the experience. He returns to that subject at the end of the chapter (vv. 36-40). While affirming prophecy and allowing tongues, he puts the expression of their spiritual gifts—about which some of the Corinthian Christians seem to be inordinately proud—in the context of the larger issue, which is order in worship

We live in a day of changing styles of worship. Some have replaced organ and choir with a synthesizer and a praise band. Some have discarded the hymns of the faith for choruses that have a modern beat. Sermons have become shorter and are more likely to be punctuated with illustrations from the latest popular movie than from Augustine. As I write this chapter, a major Baptist church in Texas finds itself in conflict over whether it is appropriate to raise hands in worship or not. In this day of changing styles, some say, "It's about time," while others long for the good old days.

Our text reminds us that this problem has plagued the church from the beginning of Christian history. In every generation, the church has faced this challenge. For example, in their book, *The Churching of America: 1776–1990*, Roger Finke and Rodney Stark discuss the camp meetings that broke out in America at the beginning of the nineteenth century. The old mainline denominations objected vehemently to the new worship styles, while many pastors jumped on the bandwagon. Barton Stone, a pivotal figure in American religious history during that time, wrote an article about the new "religious exercises." One was the falling exercise in which the worshiper would, with a piercing scream, fall like a log on the floor and appear as dead. Another was the dancing exercise. The worshiper began with jerks. Then, after jerking a while, he would begin to dance. A variation of this was the barking exercise. A person affected with the jerks, especially in the head, would make a grunt or bark from the suddenness of the jerk. Then there was the laughing exercise where a worshiper would break out in hilarious laughter. Understandably, many of the mainline worshipers rejected these exercises as inappropriate for worship.[1]

Paul does not identify barking or grunting or falling on the floor like a log as a part of worship in the Corinthian church. Yet the problems he does identify are no less disruptive than these practices that disrupted the worship experience in what is known as the Second Great Awakening. Competition between those who speak in tongues, those who prophesy, and the uncontrolled verbal interruptions by women who feel liberated through their faith in Christ disrupt the Corinthian church and evoke Paul's concern.

What can we learn from Paul's admonition to the Corinthian church?

We must neither be afraid of or enamored with innovation in worship. When innovation causes us to stretch, sparks our interest, breaks us out of our rut, and enables us to express our love for God more effectively, we must be willing to embrace it. However, innovation for innovation's sake can divert our focus from the true purpose of worship, which is to edify or build up the church.

We must neither neglect nor be obsessed with what we get out of worship. We cannot come into the presence of a Holy God without having our lives shaped by that experience. However, the purpose of worship is not that we might be fed but that God might be honored, not that we might be edified personally but that the church might be edified. If we are primarily concerned about what we get out of worship, then we have lost sight of the true focus of worship.

We must neither shy away from nor take for granted our privilege of coming into the presence of God. The veil in the temple that marked off the Holy of Holies as the domain open only to the high priest split in two when Christ died on the cross, reminding us that all of us have equal access to God: the young as well as the old, women as well as men, people of all races, and people of all levels of spiritual maturity. Every Christian has access to God, but we must remember that he *is* God! And we must remember that the only reason we can come into his presence is because of his amazing grace. So we must come into his presence with humility, with reverence, and with gratitude, and we must avoid the things that bring disorder to the experience of worship because, as Paul reminds us in our text, *God is not a God of disorder but of peace* (v. 33).

What does all of this have to do with the Corinthian church's assignment to contextualize the gospel in their pagan, pluralistic city? Paul reminds them, and us, that contextualizing the gospel in our culture does not mean mimicking our culture. Engagement and not relevancy is our ultimate goal. The frenzied, disorderly worship of the pagans reflects the character of the pagan gods. Christians have something different to offer, something better. Our God is a God of order, a God who brings peace, and a God who wants to build up and enrich the life of every worshiper. Paul wants the worship of the Corinthian Christians to reflect this unique, orderly, life-giving God to the nonbelievers in their culture. Consequently, to reflect the character of their God properly, the Corinthian Christians should make sure everything is done decently and with order in their experiences of worship.

Note

1. Roger Finke and Rodney Stark, *The Churching of America: 1776–1990* (New Brunswick NJ: Rutgers University Press, 1992) 95.

34

The Resurrection of Christ

1 Corinthians 15:1–19

He was known in his day as Judas, the Galilean. The time was AD 6, and the location was ancient Palestine. Claiming to be the Christ, Judas inflamed the countryside with messianic fever, and thousands flocked after him, hoping he was their long-awaited messiah. But then the political leaders put Judas to death. And now, 2,000 years later, we hear nothing more about Judas, the Galilean.

Then there was Simon bar Giora. The time was AD 69. Simon rallied the people of Palestine to follow him in a plan to overthrow the Romans. More than 40,000 soldiers responded to his call and marched with him into Jerusalem, where he took temporary command. Coins have been unearthed from that period bearing Simon's image and the words—"Redemption of Zion"—suggesting that he was the long-awaited messiah. But then the Romans swept into Jerusalem and put Simon bar Giora to death. Now, 2,000 years later, we hear nothing more about Simon bar Giora.

Fast forward to the year AD 135. Another Simon, this one known as Simon bar Kochba, was hailed by his fellow Palestinians as their messiah. Again, thousands rallied to his support. Again, the hopes of the people were stirred. Again, these hopes were dashed as the Romans swept into the land and Simon bar Kochba was put to death. And now, 2,000 years later, we hear nothing more about Simon bar Kochba.

Now go to the year AD 30. Again the location is ancient Palestine. Thousands of Jews rally around a man named Jesus from the insignificant city of Nazareth. Inspired by his teaching and awed by his miraculous power, they begin to think of him as the Messiah, the one who will fulfill all the promises of God to his chosen people. He goes to Jerusalem, surrounded by his entourage, apparently to claim his rightful position as the Messiah of Israel. But the religious and political leaders combine in an amalgamation of hatred, and Jesus is put to death, just like Judas the Galilean and Simon bar Giora and Simon bar Kochba. But here is the difference. Few of us have ever heard of Judas the Galilean or Simon bar Giora or Simon bar Kochba or any of the other would-be messiahs of the first two centuries. Jesus of Nazareth, however, is a different story. People on every continent on our planet know and love Jesus, hailing him as God's Son and our Savior.

Why have these other would-be messiahs faded into oblivion, but in contrast, 2,000 years later, for millions of people on this earth, Jesus has become the name above every name? The answer to that question is the historic event described in 1 Corinthians 15. Beginning in the third verse of that chapter, the Bible says,

> For what I received I passed on to you as of first importance: that Christ died for our sins according to the Scriptures, that he was buried, that he was raised on the third day according to the Scriptures, and that he appeared to Peter, and then to the Twelve. After that, he appeared to more than five hundred of the brothers at the same time, most of whom are still living, though some have fallen asleep. Then he appeared to James, then to all the apostles, and last of all he appeared to me also, as to one abnormally born. (vv. 3-8)

The reason we know of Jesus today—not only know of him but also love him, not only love him but also worship him—is because of what happened on the third day after his death. On Good Friday, the enemies of Jesus put Jesus' limp body into the tomb and rolled the stone in front of it, thinking they were done with yet another would-be messiah. However, on Easter Sunday, the tomb became a womb that produced the Risen Christ.

Paul focuses on that historic event in our text. Notice the repeated use of "that." Scholars tell us that the repeated use of "that" is equivalent to using quotation marks, which suggests that Paul recites a formula or a creed already well established in the church by the time he writes 1 Corinthians in about AD 55. This formula develops around four facts: Jesus dies (v. 3), Jesus is buried (v. 4), Jesus arises from the grave v. 4), and then Jesus appears to his disciples (v. 5 ff.). Paul's affirmation about Jesus includes all four facts. Yet the declaration that Jesus arises from the grave stands at the heart of Paul's affirmation.

The first two facts, Jesus' death and burial, reinforce the miraculous nature of that third fact. They confirm that Jesus' resurrection is no parlor trick in which Jesus fakes his death and then reappears to simulate a resurrection. When Joseph of Arimathea and Nicodemus put Jesus' body into the cave and roll the stone in front of it, Jesus is as dead as any person whose passing we have ever grieved. Jesus died and he was buried. The final fact, Jesus' appearance to the disciples, reassures us of the evidential basis for the third fact. Jesus' physical appearance to the disciples lets us know that his resurrection is not a work of fiction created in the fertile but fearful minds of Jesus' followers. Jesus appears alive, not just to one person but to many, not just on one occasion but on several occasions. The third item in Paul's list is his central thought, his declaration that Jesus comes forth from the grave. On Friday Jesus is dead. On Sunday he is alive again. Jesus arose!

What difference does it really make?

Jesus' resurrection makes a difference, first of all, in our understanding of God. Most of us will agree that we believe in God, but what kind of God do we believe in? The resurrection reminds us that the God we believe in is a God who will never let us go, even when we go through the experience of death. God will not abandon the bodies of his beloved.

God does not remove death. Every one of us will still experience death. Death goes with the territory in this fallen world. God does not remove death. Instead, God removes death as an event that separates us from him. Do you remember how Paul expresses it in his Roman epistle? "For I am convinced that neither death nor life, neither angels nor demons, neither the present nor the future, nor any powers, neither height nor depth, nor anything else in all creation, will be able to separate us from the love of God that is in Christ Jesus our Lord" (Rom 8:37-39). Nothing will separate us from God, not even death. God will not abandon the bodies of his beloved.

Jesus' resurrection also makes a difference in our understanding of Jesus. Who is this Jesus, and what should we believe about him? The resurrection affirms that Jesus is who he claims to be—God's Son, the world's Savior, the name that is above every name, and the one in whom we can put our trust. On Good Friday, the disciples fear they have misplaced their trust. They assume Jesus lied to them and that he is not who he claimed to be. However, when they stand in the presence of the Risen Christ after his resurrection, they know that whatever Jesus says, he will do. Whatever Jesus claims, that claim is true. For us, too, the resurrection of Christ assures us that we can put our trust in him.

I heard a pastor years ago explain how often our trust has been betrayed. We thought we could trust the military, but then came Vietnam. We thought we could trust the politicians, but then came Watergate. We thought we could trust the engineers, but then came the *Challenger* disaster. We thought we could trust our broker, but then came Black Monday. We thought we could trust preachers, but then came Jimmy Swaggart. In a fallen world where broken promises and misplaced trust go with the territory, we have one person in whom we can trust, one person who will never let us down, and that is the risen Christ who in his resurrection "was declared with power to be the Son of God" (Rom 1:4). Or, to put it in the words used by the New Testament Christians, the resurrection affirms that Jesus Christ is the Lord.

Further, the resurrection of Jesus Christ makes a difference in our understanding of the world. When Jesus arises from the dead, his resurrection does not only guarantee that we will someday be raised, although that is part of the promise. Jesus' resurrection signals the beginning of something new in this world right now, a new age that has broken into this present age, a new age that has a different purpose, a different set of values, a different way of relating to others, and a different end. The New Testament makes it clear that we as Christians are to act as signposts to this new order, models of this new way of life. The greatest challenge facing the church today is to discover what it means to live under the rule of God in a secular and sometimes hostile world.

How do we know God will never let us go? How do we know we can trust Jesus? How do we know a new age has been inaugurated? We know because on that third day after his death, Jesus arose from the grave.

When our son Collin was five years old, he attended preschool at Shiloh Terrace Baptist Church in Dallas, Texas, where I served as pastor. At Easter, the director of the preschool ministry shared with the children the Easter story. Collin sat next to his best friend, Petey. The director told the children briefly about Jesus' life and then, in terms she felt the children could understand, she told them that some bad men took Jesus and put him to death. When Petey heard that some bad people killed Jesus, it shook him up, and he began to cry. At that point, Collin put his arm around his distraught friend and said, "Don't worry, Petey. He comes back in the end!"

And come back he does. On Friday, the enemies of Jesus bury him in the dark dampness of the garden tomb, but Jesus comes back in the end! That is why, 2,000 years later, Jesus is not just another of the forgotten would-be messiahs of Israel. We know instead that he is God's Son, our Savior, the Risen Christ, and the Lord of Life.

35

The Resurrection of the Dead

1 Corinthians 15:20–57

The movie *Flatliners* hit theaters in 1990. The remarkable impact of this movie did not come simply from the all-star cast: Kiefer Sutherland, Julia Roberts, Kevin Bacon, William Baldwin, and Oliver Platt, actors who continue to star in blockbuster films twenty years later. The remarkable impact of the movie came from the compelling way in which it dealt with the mystery of death and what lies beyond. A group of medical students, fascinated by the near-death experiences of some of their patients, decide to explore the mysterious realm of death themselves. With certain medical techniques, they put one member of the group into a brain-dead state for two minutes, and then they bring this person back to life. The person coming back from this near-death experience gives testimony of some kind of experience after death. Three of the others follow in the same experiment, each pushing the time limit until, finally, one of them flatlines for twelve minutes before being brought back.

Some positive testimonies come out of these near-death experiences. For example, Kevin Bacon—who begins the movie as an atheist—testifies, "I really did see something out there." But toying with death also wreaks havoc in their lives. Instead of providing certainty about life after death, the experiences of these five medical students provide confusing and conflicting conclusions.

Even after such scientific or medical attempts to explore the reality of death, the curiosity remains. Is there in fact life after death? And what will that life be like? Many of us have asked those questions, if not about our own death in the future, at least about loved ones who have died. Is there in fact life after death? And what will that life be like?

Paul addresses those questions in our text, and he takes an interesting approach. He affirms that we can know for sure what will happen in the future because of something that has already happened in the past. Paul identifies this past event in the passage we considered in the last chapter. In 1 Corinthians 15:3-8, Paul recites a formula that, by AD 55, has already become well known in the church, a formula that highlights four facts: Jesus dies (15:3), Jesus is buried (v. 4), Jesus arises from the grave (v. 4), and Jesus appears to his disciples (v. 5 ff.). All four facts are important, but, as I pointed out in the last chapter, the central fact is the declaration that Jesus arose from the grave.

Paul starts with that affirmation in our text for this chapter: *But Christ has indeed been raised from the dead* (v. 20). Paul adds that the resurrection of Christ is *the firstfruits of those who have fallen asleep* (v. 20). "Firstfruits" is an agricultural term referred to in Leviticus 23:10-11. According to that passage, each harvest time, a Jewish farmer takes samples from his crop, the "firstfruits," to the priests as an offering to the Lord. The "firstfruits" precede the main harvest and provide the assurance that the rest of the harvest will be coming. In the same way, Jesus precedes us in his bodily resurrection in order to guarantee our eventual resurrection. Jesus' resurrection is the "firstfruits" of our resurrection. How do we know that we will experience life after death? The certainty concerning this future event grows out of a past event. Jesus' resurrection in the past assures us of our resurrection in the future.

Paul develops this theme further. Jesus' resurrection in the past not only provides the proof for our future resurrection but also provides the prototype for our future resurrection. The resurrection body of Jesus provides some insights into what our resurrection bodies will be like. Paul develops this theme in the final part of 1 Corinthians 15.

First of all, our resurrection bodies will be *transformed* bodies. Our resurrection bodies will be different from the bodies we have right now. Paul makes this point using the language of agriculture: *When you sow, you do not plant the body that will be, but just a seed, perhaps of wheat or of something else* (v. 37). As the wheat stalk is different from the kernel of wheat that we plant, even so the resurrection body will be different from the physical body planted in the grave. Paul reaffirms this point in the four antitheses stated in verses 42-44. *The body that is sown is perishable, it is raised imperishable; it is sown in dishonor, it is raised in glory; it is sown in weakness, it is raised in power; it is sown a natural body, it is raised a spiritual body.* Our resurrection bodies will be different from the bodies we have now.

Yet our resurrection bodies will still be *recognizable* bodies. The plant imagery implies continuity as well as difference. Although the plant that grows is different from the seed planted, continuity also ties the seed and plant together. For example, we do not plant a kernel of corn and get an apple tree! In the same way, some continuity will connect our physical bodies and our resurrection bodies. I remember a preacher saying, "What is vital to a person as person will be raised in a spiritual body." Our resurrection bodies will be recognizable bodies, maybe more so by what we are and by what we say and by what we do than by what we look like.

Our resurrection bodies will also be *incorruptible* bodies. Our physical bodies are corruptible. They are subject to decay. We are in the process of dying every day, but our resurrection bodies will be removed from this realm of decay. Paul emphasizes this idea in his description of Jesus' resurrection body. In verse 4 and then again in verse 12, when Paul affirms that Jesus has been raised from the dead, he uses the perfect tense, which is the Greek way of stating a past action that has a continuing impact in the present. When Jesus is raised from the dead, his body is transformed so that it can never die again. Our resurrection bodies will be like that. They will never be subject to decay or death or dissolution. They will be incorruptible.

Further, our resurrection bodies will be *powerful* bodies. In verse 43, Paul alludes to the weaknesses of our physical bodies. We are limited in so many ways. But our resurrection bodies will be free from all the limitations and handicaps that we now know. At that point, we will be able to measure up to the highest potential of God's plan and purpose for us.

Finally, our resurrection bodies will be *adequate* bodies. Our resurrection bodies will be adequate to function in the new realm of existence in which we will live through all eternity. In both this life and in the next, we have bodies. Paul modifies the word "body" with two adjectives: "natural" and "spiritual." Just as God has given us natural bodies adequate to live in this life, even so God will give us spiritual bodies adequate to exist in the next life.

How does Paul know these things about our future resurrection bodies? Where does this description of our future resurrection bodies come from? It comes from the descriptions of the resurrected body of Jesus, a body so transformed that the disciples on the Emmaus road do not realize this is Jesus, and yet a body eventually recognizable by his words and his deeds. Jesus' resurrection body is an incorruptible body that ascends to be with the Father, a powerful body that can pass through a closed door and suddenly appear to the disciples, and an adequate body that is now at the right hand of the Father interceding on our behalf. Jesus' resurrection is both the proof and prototype for our resurrection. In both cases, we can correctly describe the future based on an event that occurs in the past.

How should we respond to this news that Jesus' resurrection is both the proof and prototype of our future resurrection? How should we respond to this news that there is indeed life after death? It is at this point that we see the greatest divergence between the movie, *Flatliners,* and the Scripture. The awareness of life after death for those in the movie creates havoc and fear and despair. But notice Paul's response in our text. After assuring us that we too will be raised, just like Jesus was, he bursts into a dramatic doxology: *But thanks be to God! He gives us the victory through our Lord Jesus Christ* (v. 57). Death is not the end of the sentence of life but merely a comma that will punctuate our lives with a greater significance. *Thanks be to God!* Those whom we have lost to the experience of death are in fact more alive now than they have ever been. *Thanks be to God!* Death does not end our relationships with those whom we love, for someday we will be united with them in the eternal fellowship we call heaven. *Thanks be to God!* Our future is not clouded with uncertainty, for we have this assurance from God's word: someday we will be reunited with Jesus and will see God face to face. *Thanks be to God!*

36

The Interception of Entropy

1 Corinthians 15:58

At a leadership seminar, one of the panelists was Max DePree. Max DePree was at that time the chairman emeritus of Herman Miller office furniture manufacturer, one of the most innovative and admired companies in America. He is also a member of *Fortune Magazine's* Business Hall of Fame and a best-selling author. During a question-and-answer period, one of the analysts asked him, "What is one of the most difficult things that you personally need to work on?" DePree answered, "The interception of entropy."[1]

We know what it means to intercept something. During a war, we try to intercept messages. During a ball game, we try to intercept a pass. We know what it means to intercept something, but what does it mean to intercept *entropy*? What is entropy? Entropy is the tendency of an energy system to run down. It happens to basketball teams who run out of energy and let victory slip from their grasp in the closing seconds of the game, like the Dallas Mavericks did in the 2005 National Basketball Association finals. Entropy! It happens to businesses. In 1982, Thomas Peters and Robert Waterman wrote a book titled *In Search of Excellence* in which they listed seventy-five companies that had achieved excellence. But then, over the next few years, three-fourths of those companies failed either partially or completely. Entropy!

Entropy also happens to people. Some years ago, a top Christian leader disqualified himself from ministry. A journalist described his demise in these words: "He sank like a rock, beat up, burned out, angry and depressed, no good to himself and no good to the people he loved." A while later, when the pastor himself wrote about his experience, he explained, "Many people still wonder whatever happened to me. They think I had a crisis of faith. The fact is I simply collapsed on the inside." Entropy![2]

Entropy happens to everyone. Therefore, businessman Max De Pree declared that his most important responsibility as a leader is to intercept the entropy that inevitably comes in an organization or on a team or in a person.

Paul recognizes the need to intercept entropy in the Corinthian church. I believe that is why he concludes his letter to the Corinthian church, in which he deals with one problem after another, with the affirmation that Jesus Christ has risen from the dead and that his resurrection is both the proof and the prototype of our future resurrection. Paul wants to intercept the entropy that has settled on the Corinthian church. He wants to shore up the Corinthian Christians who are dangerously close to collapsing on the inside. He wants to prevent the Corinthian Christians from giving out and giving up.

He gives this word of encouragement to the Corinthians and to us: *Therefore, my dear brothers, stand firm. Let nothing move you. Always give yourselves fully to the work of the Lord, because you know that your labor in the Lord is not in vain.* Paul's challenge contains two dimensions—a passive one and an active one.

We see the passive dimension in the opening words of the challenge: *Stand firm. Let nothing move you* (v. 58). To stand firm means to face our challenge rather than running from it. To stand firm means to hold on rather than giving up. The early Christians understood that. Their persistence explains why, in the catacombs beneath the ancient Roman Coliseum, where the early Christians waited before being put to death, they not only engraved on the wall the symbol of the cross but also the symbol of the anchor. When the storms of death blew, they had something that held them in the wind, something in which they could anchor their lives and find stability. Paul wants to see that same kind of persistence in the Corinthian Christians. *Stand firm. Let nothing move you,* he challenges. That is the passive dimension.

But then Paul adds this active dimension to the challenge: *Always give yourselves fully to the work of the Lord.* The key words in this part of the challenge are "give" and "work"—active words that picture an energetic effort. Standing firm is sometimes not enough.

William Booth, the founder of the Salvation Army, understood that. Toward the end of his life, Booth lost sight in both eyes. When the doctor told him the loss was permanent, that they could do nothing to recover his sight, Booth replied, "I have done what I could for God and for the people with my eyes. Now I shall do what I can without my eyes."[3] Just standing firm was not enough for William Booth. He wanted to continue doing the work of the Lord.

Paul echoes the same thoughts in this challenge to the Corinthian Christians. *Always give yourselves fully to the work of the Lord,* Paul tells the Corinthian Christians. That is the active dimension. Paul wants to intercept entropy in the Corinthian church, so he sends them this challenge. Let nothing move you, and let nothing stop you. Hold on and then move forward.

But why should we hold on and then move forward? Why not just give up? Why not just let entropy have its way? We see two answers in our text, one at the beginning of the verse and the other at the end of the verse.

Paul begins with the word, "Therefore." That word suggests our first incentive. Like an arrow, "therefore" points back to the passage that precedes it, and in the preceding passage Paul has reminded the Corinthian Christians of all the things God has done for them. God has provided salvation through Christ. God has won the victory over death. God has given a purpose to live for. God has given a power to live by. God has offered the hope of a future resurrection. "Therefore," because of what God has done for us, Paul affirms, we should stand firm in our faith and keep doing the work of the Lord.

We find the other incentive at the end of the verse where Paul writes, *because you know that your labor in the Lord is not in vain.* Paul reminds the Corinthian Christians that what they do for God in the everyday ebb and flow of their Christian lives will make a difference in this world. We can see evidences of that truth in our lives today as well.

A few years back I received a call from a pastor in Alabama. He told me he called to tell me thanks, and then he explained. He had seen my name printed somewhere—with my location—so he tracked me down. He reminded me of a youth rally where I preached in Pensacola, Florida, in about 1980. He told me that during my invitation, I challenged those to come forward who were willing to respond to God's call in their lives. He told me he came forward that night, and then he said he had never taken time to thank me for my influence in his life. I did not remember his name. I did not remember the service. I did not remember what I had said. Yet somehow I had influenced his life, and he called to tell me thanks.

Paul makes the same point in our text. No matter how small or insignificant, every word we say and every deed we do for the Lord will have eternal consequences. *Our labor for the Lord is not in vain.* Because of what God has done for us, and because of the impact of what we do for him, we like the Corinthian Christians should stand firm in our faith and keep doing the work of the Lord.

But let me offer this word of warning: standing firm and moving forward in the work of the Lord will not be easy. It has never been easy to stand firm in the midst of opposition, and it has never been easy to move forward in the midst of obstacles. It has never been easy to keep doing the work of the Lord. We must be honest about the difficulty of our challenge. We must face the brutal facts about the difficulty of contextualizing the gospel in this fallen world.

In his book *From Good to Great*, Jim Collins offers an unforgettable illustration of the need to face facts honestly when he introduces what he calls the Stockdale Paradox. This concept emanates from the experience of Admiral Jim Stockdale, who was the highest-ranking United States military officer in the "Hanoi Hilton" prisoner-of-war camp during the height of the Vietnam War. Tortured over twenty times during his eight-year imprisonment from 1965 to 1973, Stockdale nevertheless survived. He stood firm, and then he eventually moved forward. When Jim Collins interviewed Admiral Stockdale, the admiral said, "I never lost faith in the end of the story. I never doubted not only that I would get out, but also that I would prevail in the end and turn the experience into the defining moment of my life."

They walked in silence for a few moments, with Stockdale limping and arc-swinging his stiff leg that had never fully recovered from repeated torture. Finally, Collins asked him, "Who didn't make it out?"

"Oh, that's easy," the admiral answered. "The optimists."

"I don't understand," Collins replied. "What do you mean by 'the optimists'?"

The admiral explained, "The optimists were the ones who said, 'We're going to be out by Christmas.' And Christmas would come, and Christmas would go. Then they'd say, 'We're going to be out by Easter.' And Easter would come, and Easter would go. And then Thanksgiving, and then it would be Christmas again. And they died of a broken heart."

Silence again prevailed for a few minutes. Finally, the admiral broke the silence. He turned to Collins and said, "This is a very important lesson. You must never confuse faith that you will prevail in the end—which you can never afford to lose—with the discipline to confront the most brutal facts of your current reality, whatever they might be."

"To this day," Jim Collins testified, "I carry a mental image of Stockdale admonishing the optimists: 'We're not getting out by Christmas; deal with it!'"[4]

We need to carry that image with us as we try to contextualize the church in our twenty-first-century pluralistic, postmodern world. It might be the one thing that will enable us to make it through without giving up or giving out. Life is tough. Deal with it. People will disappoint us. Deal with it. We will have to struggle against temptation until we breathe our last breath. Deal with it. Things will happen that we cannot comprehend. Deal with it. The church will never fully meet our expectations. Deal with it. Our pastor will sometimes disappoint us. Deal with it. Some people will laugh at us when we talk to them about Jesus. Deal with it. We will have moments in our lives when the ever-present God might appear to be a silent God. Deal with it. We are not getting out by Christmas. Deal with it. We need to understand that brutal fact clearly.

But then we need to remember this encouraging promise that will keep us going: *Therefore, my dear brothers, stand firm. Let nothing move you. Always give yourselves fully to the work of the Lord, because you know that your labor in the Lord is not in vain.*

Notes

1. Max De Pree, *Leadership Is an Art* (New York: Dell Publishing, 1989) 110.

2. Bill Hybels, *Courageous Leadership* (Grand Rapids MI: Zondervan, 2002) 184–85.

3. David Bennett, *William Booth* (Minneapolis MN: Bethany House Publishers, 1986) 184.

4. Jim Collins, *Good to Great* (New York: Harper Business, 2001) 83–85.

37

What's the Deal with the Offering Plates?

1 Corinthians 16:1-4

A new member of the church—he had only been a member for a couple of Sundays—asked the pastor as he left, "What's the deal with the offering plates?" Not knowing exactly where he was going with his question, the pastor responded, "What do you mean?" The new member explained, "I have no clue how this whole thing works. I want to do what God wants me to do, but I don't know how it works. Who is supposed to give, and how often, and how much?"

That conversation could be repeated in most churches today. We assume that everyone who comes to church knows what the Bible teaches concerning giving to the church, but they really do not. Many people who attend our church every Sunday might well voice the question, "What's the deal with the offering plates?"

Apparently some in the Corinthian church confront Paul with that same question: "What's the deal with the offering plates?" Paul responds to that question in our text. He begins by calling on the Christians at Corinth to do what he told the Galatian churches to do (v. 1). We do not know what Paul told the Galatian churches to do, for we have no record of it. Paul says nothing like this in the New Testament letter known as Galatians, so it must be something he told them in person. In case the Corinthian Christians do not know what he told the Galatian Christians, Paul repeats it in his instructions to them. His instructions concerning giving are clear, to the point, and practical.

In our text, of course, Paul specifically addresses an offering to meet the needs of the Christians back in Jerusalem who are going through a difficult time as they share the gospel. We can probably feel comfortable, however, in applying his instructions to giving in general. For those who want to know, "What's the deal with the offering plates?" Paul provides some answers.

Paul first affirms that our giving should be *personal*. Paul instructs the Corinthians, *Each one of you should set aside a sum of money* (v. 2). Nowhere in the Bible are any of God's children excluded from the requirement of giving. On the contrary, the clear teaching of Scripture is that as a part of our worship of God, each of us should bring our offering to him. In the Old Testament, we hear the resounding challenge of the prophet Malachi to all of God's children: "Bring the whole tithe into the storehouse" (Mal 3:10). In the New Testament, we hear the comprehensive command of the Apostle Paul: "Each man should give what he has decided in his heart to give, not reluctantly or under compulsion, for God loves a cheerful giver" (2 Cor 9:7).

God expects every Christian to give. God expects both new Christians and mature Christians to give. God expects both young Christians and older Christians to give. God expects both married adults and single adults to give. God expects both children and young people to give. God expects both those who have much and those who have little to give.

So what's the deal with the offering plates? Paul reminds us that "each one of you should set aside a sum of money." Giving is to be personal.

Then Paul adds that our giving should be *purposeful*. We are to give, Paul suggests, "on the first day of every week." By the time Paul writes this letter to the church at Corinth, Christians are meeting for worship on the first day of every week. Paul simply suggests that every time they gather with other Christians to worship, a regular part of their expression of faith and devotion to God should be the giving of an offering.

Every time the offering plate passes in front of us, we are reminded that our giving should be disciplined and intentional. We should not wait until someone begs us to give. We should not wait until all our other bills are paid to give. We should not wait until the end of the year to give. We should not wait to see what others do to give. We should not wait until the church's budget gets behind to give. We should not wait until we have enough money to give. Instead, week by week, in a purposeful way, we are to give our offerings to the Lord. Giving is to be purposeful.

Paul further instructs that our giving should be *proportional*. When we give, Paul writes that each of them should set aside a sum of money from their wages. Jesus underscores this principle when he declares, "From everyone who has been given much, much will be demanded" (Luke 12:48). Jesus also demonstrates his understanding of this principle when he concludes that the widow in the temple who places in the offering plate only two small coins while the wealthy worshipers fill the plates with their coins "has put in more than all the others" (Luke 21:3). How can Jesus make such a statement? He explains, "All these people gave their gifts out of their wealth; but she out of her poverty put in all she had to live on" (Luke 21:4). It is not the amount of money we give but the amount of money we have left that determines the value of our gift. To use a slogan many churches have used in capital campaigns, "Not equal gifts but equal sacrifice." Our giving should be proportional.

Let us return to the question raised by the new Christian in the story I told to begin this chapter and see if we have some answers to give. "I have no clue how this whole thing works," this new member said. "I want to do what God wants me to do, but I don't know how it works. Who is supposed to give, and how often, and how much?"

Who is supposed to give? Paul clearly includes everyone. Everyone is supposed to give. When we become part of the body of Christ, then we are responsible to support that body. Or, to put it another way, when we are a part of a church and benefit from the ministries of that church, then we are responsible to support the ministries through our financial contributions.

How often are we to give? Paul suggests a regular pattern of giving that recognizes giving as part of our experience of worship. We are not to give haphazardly or grudgingly but deliberately and joyfully.

How much should we give? We should give proportionate to what we have. Some people give a set amount each week or each month, the same amount year in and year out. That is certainly better than not giving at all. However, if that amount does not fluctuate according to the fluctuations of our income, then we are not following Paul's instructions concerning giving. Paul suggests a proportional approach so that as the income increases, our giving will increase.

A cartoon shows a pastor telling his congregation, "I've always preached that the poor were welcome in this church. Now I see by the offering the past few Sundays that they have been coming!" Being poor materially is not a sin, but to be poor in spirit and poor in compassion and poor in commitment to Christ is a problem. The tragedy of today's church is that too many believers put a dollar in the plate when they are at church, when they feel like it, when they like what is happening, and when they don't have any other plan for that dollar. In contrast, Paul asserts, our giving is to be personal and purposeful and proportionate.

What should we do in response to this clear teaching of the Bible? Let me recall a story out of the lore of Texas history. Most Texans recognize the name Sam Houston, for he is, in a sense, the father of Texas. In 1840, when he married Margaret Lea of Alabama, he was not a Christian. Instead, his legendary drinking bouts and penchant for fighting earned him the nickname "Big Drunk." But Margaret prayed for him and witnessed to him consistently. Finally, at the age of sixty-three, Houston made his public confession of faith at the Independence Baptist Church.

Paul Powell describes the special moment in these words:

> On November 19, 1854, with hundreds of people gathered around, Houston waded into the chilly waters of Little Rocky Creek to be baptized by Rufus C. Burleson, pastor of the Independence Baptist Church and president of Baylor University....When asked if he wanted to put away his fine leather wallet before entering the water, Houston declined, insisting that it be baptized as well. So it was that in Little Rocky Creek, with its clear water streaming over limestone and banks lined with stately oaks, 'one of the greatest religious leaders of early Texas baptized the greatest political leader of early Texas, wallet and all.'

When that happens to us—when we are really baptized in the Spirit of Christ, wallet and all—we will understand that our money does not belong to us but instead belongs to God. We will all then give to the work of God's kingdom through his church, personally and purposefully and proportionately. We will also realize that our money is not a barometer of our worth but is instead a conduit for ministry. When we do that we will experience what Jesus once said: "It is more blessed to give than to receive" (Acts 20:35). When that happens, then we will have the resources we need to contextualize the church in our twenty-first-century world.

Note

1. Paul Powell, *Back to Bedrock: Messages on our Historic Baptist Faith* (Dallas: Baptistway Press, 2003) 129–30.

38

Opportunities and Obstacles

1 Corinthians 16:5-12

It is an opportunity of a lifetime, and if he manipulates the pieces of the puzzle precisely, he will accomplish his lifetime dream. That premise runs like a thread through *The Da Vinci Code*, first published in 2003. The man who has this once-in-a-lifetime opportunity is an anonymous seeker mysteriously known as the Teacher. The dream for which he has waited a lifetime is of finding the Holy Grail. At just the right moment, the Teacher initiates the strategy that will bring into his possession this long-desired holy relic. However, realizing his dream turns out to be more difficult than he thinks. One uncovered secret leads to yet another secret to be uncovered. The Priory of Sion, a secret society whose members have been hiding the Holy Grail for centuries, deceives him. Robert Langdon, a Harvard symbologist, and Sophie Neveu, a gifted French cryptologist, prove to be formidable opponents as well. The mistakes of the Teacher's handpicked associates continually add complexity to the circumstances. In a frantic race that begins in Paris and ends in London, the Teacher sees his opportunity gradually slip away from him.[1] That popular book of fiction—and I underscore that it is fiction—provides a parable of what life is like for all of us most of the time. We have plentiful opportunities, but many obstacles stand in our way.

The Apostle Paul experiences the same juxtaposition of opportunities and obstacles, as he clearly reveals in our text for this chapter. Even though Paul founded the Corinthian church, he now finds himself in an adversarial relationship with some of the leaders of the church. Some of them do not even want Paul to visit Corinth, nor do they want his lackey, Timothy, to visit as his representative. They prefer Apollos, and a rumor insinuates that Paul refuses to let Apollos come. Paul addresses these issues in our text. What catches my attention in this text is the statement in verse 9, for it identifies two dynamics that always appear in every experience of every life: opportunity and obstacles. *A great door for effective work has opened to me*, Paul declares in verse 9, *and there are many who oppose me*.

Think of Paul's situation. He writes this letter to the Corinthian Christians from the city of Ephesus. What golden opportunities Paul has in Ephesus! Luke describes these opportunities in Acts 19 where he concludes, "God did extraordinary miracles through Paul" (Acts 19:11). So powerful is Paul's influence there in Ephesus that the local citizens use the handkerchiefs he touches to heal some who are sick. So convincing is Paul's message that many who practice magic burn their books so they can follow the true God. What a wide-open door of opportunity Paul has in Ephesus. Yet many obstacles stand in the way, for in this very city Demetrius and the silversmiths rally the crowds against Paul to such a degree that he has to leave. Paul experiences an open door for effective work *and* many adversaries.

That paradoxical combination of opportunity and opposition still surfaces today. For example, Fred DeLuca began a series of sandwich shops that have become the Subway franchise. With more than 34,000 Subway stores in ninety-six countries, we can conclude that Fred DeLuca was certainly a man who knew how to take advantage of his opportunities. Yet, from the beginning, obstacles stood in his way. When he opened his first store, he had never even made a sandwich. So his first obstacle was to figure out how to make a submarine sandwich. Then the first store almost shut down because of declining sales. Did he quit? No. He opened a second store. The concept began to develop, but it took him ten years to expand to twenty-five stores. It took him twenty-two years to build the first 1,000 stores. Did he take advantage of his opportunities? With spades! Was it easy? Of course not. DeLuca says, "Regardless of the year, we faced challenges each and every week."[2] Fred DeLuca experienced a great door for effective work *and* many adversaries.

Opportunities and obstacles come together for the Apostle Paul in the first-century city of Ephesus and also for Fred DeLuca in the twentieth century. So why do we think it will be any different for us individually as we establish our relationships and build our families and pursue our career goals? Why do we think it will be any different for our church as we seek to contextualize the gospel in our community? Do we think the world exists just to satisfy our desires and make life comfortable for us? Do we think if our church speaks, the world will automatically listen? As we pursue the opportunities God has placed before us, as individuals and as a church, some people will misunderstand us, some will oppose us, and some will simply ignore us. Opportunities and obstacles always go together.

Someone once said, "Whenever you hear everything is going as planned, somebody is either a fool or a liar."[3] Or, in more graphic terms, another quip suggests, "When your cup runneth over, looketh out!" This principle is inescapably ingrained in the fabric of life: a great door for effective work *and* many adversaries.

What will it take for us to move around these obstacles and overcome the opposition so that we can fulfill the opportunities God gives to us as individuals and as a church? The starting point is purpose. We must be clear about what kind of person and what kind of church we want to be. In his book, *The 7 Habits of Highly Effective People*, Stephen R. Covey suggests that effective people "begin with the end in mind." That means, he explains, we start with a clear understanding of our destiny. He adds, "The most effective way I know to begin with the end in mind is to develop a *personal mission statement*."[4]

Do we have a personal mission statement? Do we know what we want to do with our lives? Do we have a clear focus on where we want to go? Without a personal mission statement—that is, without a purpose—we will end up being like the man about whom it was said, "He mounted his horse and rode off in all directions!" We must be clear about what kind of person we want to be, and the same thing is true of our church.

This is why the Acts 1:8 model for the church must recapture the church today. The Acts 1:8 model gives us a purpose—a biblical purpose, a worthy purpose, a challenging purpose—for it reminds us that our church has the responsibility to take the gospel from our front door to the ends of the earth. That purpose should determine our priorities as a church. That purpose should dominate our conversations as church members.

We must then have a passion for pursuing that purpose. Former Olympic gold medalist Mary Lou Retton said, "Every great achievement is the story of a flaming heart."[5] She is right. The reason some individuals transform opportunities into realized dreams, while others are stymied by the obstacles that stand in the way, is that they care more about fulfilling their purpose. They have passion. The reason some churches transform the opportunities God gives them into significant kingdom achievement, while others flounder around until they die, is that they care more about fulfilling their purpose. They have passion. "Every great achievement is the story of a flaming heart."

As a final ingredient, we must add persistence. The opposition that stands in our way will not give up. Neither must we. The obstacles that block the pathway to our goals will not go away. Neither must we.

The 1993 movie titled *Rudy* tells the story of a young man named Rudy Ruettiger who grows up in a steel mill town where most people end up working in the mills. But he has a dream. He dreams of playing football at Notre Dame. Yet some problems loom large before him. To begin with, his grades are too low for him to get into Notre Dame. In addition, his athletic skills are too poor for him to play at Notre Dame. Finally, he is about half the size of the other players. Nevertheless, Rudy pursues his purpose with a passion and with persistence until finally, at the end of the film, he gets into the game, makes a tackle, and is carried off the field by his fellow players. Just before the game, someone asks him, "Are you ready for this, Rudy?" Rudy responds, "I've been ready for this all my life." The film recounts the amazing story of an impossible dream that is turned into a reality by a person willing to pursue it passionately and persistently.

Some day, when we stand before God and give an account to him of what we have done with our lives and what we have done in the church, imagine if we say, "But God, there were so many obstacles in the way, and so many people who opposed me. It was just too hard." Do you think God will understand?

Notes

1. Dan Brown, *The Da Vinci Code* (New York: Doubleday, 2003).

2. Fred DeLuca, *Start Small Finish Big* (New York: Warner Books, 2000) 27–49.

3. Theodore Levitt, *Thinking about Management* (New York: The Free Press, 1991) 45.

4. Stephen R. Covey, *The 7 Habits of Highly Effective People* (New York: Simon and Schuster, 1989) 106.

5. Mary Lou Retton, *Mary Lou Retton's Gateways to Happiness* (New York: Broadway Books, 2000) 135.

39

A Door into a New World

1 Corinthians 16:13–22

Although Thomas Merton writes out of the context of his life in the Catholic church, his books, especially the *Seven Story Mountain,* have touched the lives of people all over the world, Catholic and Protestant alike. Born in 1915, he spent his first two decades in self-indulgence. The unexpected pregnancy of one of his girlfriends forced him to consider the consequences of his delinquent behavior. He went to America to live with his grandparents and make a fresh start. While he was running away, he ran into God. It happened in 1938, when Merton was twenty-three years old. One Sunday morning, instead of taking his usual trip to Long Island to see a girlfriend, he decided to go to mass for the first time in his life. He went to the Corpus Christi Church near Harlem. After the service began, Merton felt uncomfortable because he was unfamiliar with the rituals of the Catholic service. But he stayed and tried to follow along, listening to the priest's homily, watching the activities going on around him. After mass, he left the church filled with a strange, new joy. He later wrote, "I could not understand what . . . had happened to make me so happy, why I was so much at peace, so content with life. . . . All I know is that I walked in a new world!"[1]

What an incredible picture of what the church should be—not just a building where people meet, not just an organization that gets things done, and not just an institution that houses ancient documents, but a place where people discover a new way of looking at life. The church should be a door into a new world.

That is Paul's dream for the Corinthian church. Paul wants the church in Corinth to be an island of faith in the middle of a pagan city where Christ intersects with culture through Christians who incarnate the gospel in their environment to provide a door into a new world. But from the beginning, the Corinthian Christians have a difficult time being that kind of church in the world because they cannot seem to keep the world out of the church. Paul pens this letter called 1 Corinthians to instruct them and inspire them to be the church. In our text for this final chapter, Paul comes to the end of his epistle. Often we gloss over these final words without giving them much attention. After all, we surmise, this passage contains the words with which a person customarily closes a letter to friends in the first-century world. On closer scrutiny, we find that Paul's closing words contain extraordinary insights into how the church of the first century and the church of the twenty-first century can be a door into a new world.

To begin with, Paul reminds the Corinthian Christians that this new world of the church is much bigger than their own experience of it. We often become so bogged down in our own local church situation that we lose sight of the bigger picture. That probably happens to the Christians at Corinth. Things are not going well in Corinth. Everywhere they turn, obstacles and opposition confront them. "What is the use?" they might mumble to themselves. "The church is not making much of a difference in the world." In the closing words of this letter, Paul reminds them that the church is bigger than their own experience of it.

In verse 17, Paul mentions *Stephanas, Fortunatus, and Achaicus* and the other Christians at Achai (v. 17). In verse 19, he alludes to *the churches in the province of Asia* and *Aquila and Priscilla,* and *the church that meets at their house.* All of these people are a part of the church. The New Testament at times speaks of the church located in particular places like the church at Jerusalem (Acts 5:11) and the church at Antioch (13:1) and the church at Caesarea (18:22). This is the local church. Yet, at the same time, the New Testament writers also speak of a church that consists of all believers in all local churches (1 Cor 10:32; Col 1:18; 1 Tim 3:15; especially Ephesians), because they want us to recognize that the church of Jesus Christ is bigger than our own local church.

Patrick Johnstone, a spokesman on the mission of the church today, authored the book *The Church Is Bigger than You Think.* In the introduction, he gives three reasons for writing the book. He wants to show that the church is bigger than we think in terms of *time*. God planned the church in eternity before time began, and its destiny is to be with God for all eternity when time is no more. Incredibly, he has given us the privilege of being part of that eternal body. Johnstone also wants to show that the church is bigger than we think in terms of *size*. He charts in his book the amazing expansion of the church in all its variety and ministries in the twentieth century. Incredibly, we are a part of that growth. He also wants to show that the church is bigger than we think in terms of *structure*. Our perception of what constitutes the structures of the church is often based on inadequate theology and distorted patterns, according to Johnstone, causing many churches to be marginalized in the call to world evangelism. We need to adopt a structure, Johnstone claims, that will enable us to accomplish the goal of "a church of every people and the gospel for every person."[2]

If we can begin to understand the bigness of the church, the vast scope of the church's ministry, and the eternal dimension of the church's destiny, then when people connect with our church it will be like walking into a new world.

This new world of the church is also a place where leadership is given on the basis of service rendered. In these closing verses, Paul twice mentions a man named Stephanos and his household. Stephanos is one of the first converts of Paul in his mission to Achaia, and in fact Stephanos is one of the few Paul baptizes himself. Stephanos obviously positions himself as one of Paul's supporters. Therefore, if Paul simply commands the Corinthians to follow the leadership of Stephanos because he is Paul's supporter, the Corinthians, especially those who oppose Paul, will reject him. So notice what Paul does. Paul points to the ministry Stephanos has carried out and asserts that by his ministry Stephanos has earned the right to be a leader. Literally, what Paul says in verse 15 is this: *They have appointed themselves for service (diakonia) to the saints.*

That should be the pattern of every church—leadership proffered on the basis of service rendered. You say you have a Ph.D. in organizational management—so what? You say you have been elected deacon of the church—so what? You say you have been a member of the church for fifty years—so what? You say you give more money to the church than anyone else—so what? You say the church called you to be a minister on the staff—so what? Leadership in the church of Jesus Christ does not come by education or position or seniority or personality. It comes on the basis of service. If we want to be leaders in the church, we should earn it. In the church of Jesus Christ, a person does not *rise* to leadership; she *descends* to leadership as she rolls up her sleeves and becomes involved in ministry.

Do you remember how Jesus put it? "You know that those who are regarded as rulers of the Gentiles lord it over them, and their high officials exercise authority over them. Not so with you. Instead, whoever wants to become great among you must be your servant, and whoever wants to be first must be slave of all" (Mark 10:42-44). If we can be that kind of church, where leadership is given on the basis of service rendered, connecting with our church will be like walking into a new world.

Paul further reminds the Corinthian Christians that this new world of the church is a place where people genuinely care for one another. Notice the warmth of Paul's words in verses 19 and 20: *The churches in the province of Asia send you greetings. Aquila and Priscilla greet you warmly in the Lord, and so does the church that meets at their house. All the brothers here send you greetings. Greet one another with a holy kiss.*

Well-known preacher Fred Craddock says that his mother took him to church as a boy, but his father did not go. In fact, his father complained about Sunday dinner being late when she came home. Sometimes the preacher came to see him, and Craddock's father would say, "I know what the church wants. The church doesn't care about me. The church wants another name, another pledge. Right? Isn't that the name of it? Another name, another pledge." When the church had a revival, the pastor always brought the evangelist by to see Fred's dad. And Fred's dad would say the same thing. He would look at the evangelist and say, "The church doesn't care about me. The church just wants another name and another pledge." Then, years later, Fred's father was in the hospital. He had lost weight and was down to seventy-three pounds. His throat was irreparably scarred from radiation. He was near death. Fred flew in to see him, and when he walked in he saw potted plants and cut flowers all over the room and a stack of cards twenty inches deep beside his father's bed. All the flowers and every card and every potted plant came from a person or group from the church. Fred picked up some of the cards and began to read them. His father was not able to speak, but he took a Kleenex box and wrote on it a line from Shakespeare. These were the words: "In this harsh world, draw your breath in pain to tell my story." Fred asked, "What is your story, Daddy?" And Fred's dad wrote, "I was wrong. They do care."[3] When we genuinely care for each other like that, then connecting with our church will be like walking into a new world.

Also, this new world of the church is a place where people recognize Jesus as the Christ. Paul's abrupt ending to his letter to the Corinthians is startling. In verse 21, Paul picks up the pen himself. He has been dictating the letter to a secretary up to this point, but he closes this letter, as he often does, by scratching out a final word in his own hand. What does Paul say in this final word? How does he follow up the warmth of verses 19 and 20? He writes, *If anyone does not love the Lord—a curse be on him* (v. 22). Why does Paul feel the need to pronounce a curse on those who do not share his passion for Jesus Christ? Paul believes that a commitment to Jesus Christ is at the heart of the church's life. Unless we believe in Jesus, we are not the church. Unless we follow Jesus, we are not the church.

It is not enough to have a vision as big as the world. It is not enough to serve other people. It is not enough to love one another. We can actually do all of those things and still not be the church. We can do all of those things and still not offer to the world a door into a new world. Jesus declares, "I am the door; if anyone enters through Me, he shall be saved, and shall go in and out, and find pasture" (John 10:9, NASB). We must go through that door, Jesus, to get to the new world.

A young lady named Noella came to the front during the invitation one Sunday when I was the pastor of the First Baptist Church in Richardson. She told me about a pastor and his wife in Missouri who introduced her to Jesus and helped her understand what it means to become a Christian. She told me that she is now sharing her story with a friend. She told the friend, "You can't get to the Father except through the Son." Noella is exactly right. Jesus is the one who forgives sins. Jesus is the one who brings salvation. Jesus is the one who gives life. Jesus is the one who connects us with the Father. Jesus is the one who guarantees our future. If we don't believe in Jesus, we will all be cursed because we can't get to the Father except through the Son.

Can we really be that kind of church—a church that recognizes a bigger reality than we ourselves have experienced, a church where people genuinely care for one another, a church where leadership is given on the basis of service rendered, and a place where Jesus Christ is believed and followed? If we can be that kind of church, then maybe someday another twenty-three-year-old young man looking for meaning for his life, like Thomas Merton, can worship with us and then, when he leaves, give this testimony to his friends: "I could not understand what it was that happened to make me so happy, why I was so much at peace, so content with life. . . . All I know is that I walked in a new world!" Wouldn't that be incredible?

Notes

1. Jennifer Fisher Bryant, *Thomas Merton: Poet, Prophet, Priest* (Grand Rapids MI: Wm B. Eerdmans Publishing, 1997) 80–81.

2. Patrick Johnstone, *The Church Is Bigger than You Think* (Pasadena CA: William Carey Library Publishers, 1998) 9–10.

3. Fred B. Craddock, *Craddock Stories* (St. Louis MO: Chalice Press, 2001) 14.

www.ingramcontent.com/pod-product-compliance
Lightning Source LLC
Chambersburg PA
CBHW062207080426
42734CB00010B/1830